ACE YOUR SHRM CERTIFICATION EXAM
SECOND EDITION

Ace Your SHRM Certification Exam

Second Edition

The *Official* SHRM Study Guide for the
SHRM-CP® and SHRM-SCP® Exams

Plus 40 SHRM-CP/SHRM-SCP Practice Items

Editors Alexander Alonso, Ph.D., SHRM-SCP
and Nancy A. Woolever, SHRM-SCP

Society for Human Resource Management
Alexandria, Virginia shrm.org

Society for Human Resource Management, India Office
Mumbai, India shrmindia.org

Society for Human Resource Management, Middle East and Africa Office
Dubai, UAE shrm.org/about-shrm/pages/shrm-mena.aspx

BETTER WORKPLACES
BETTER WORLD™

This publication is designed to provide accurate and authoritative information regarding the subject matter covered. It is sold with the understanding that neither the publisher nor the author is engaged in rendering legal or other professional service. If legal advice or other expert assistance is required, the services of a competent, licensed professional should be sought. The federal and state laws discussed in this book are subject to frequent revision and interpretation by amendments or judicial revisions that may significantly affect employer or employee rights and obligations. Readers are encouraged to seek legal counsel regarding specific policies and practices in their organizations.

This book is published by SHRM, the Society for Human Resource Management. The interpretations, conclusions, and recommendations in this book are those of the author and do not necessarily represent those of the publisher.

SHRM, the Society for Human Resource Management, creates better workplaces where employers and employees thrive together. As the voice of all things work, workers, and the workplace, SHRM is the foremost expert, convener, and thought leader on issues impacting today's evolving workplaces. With 300,000+ HR and business executive members in 165 countries, SHRM impacts the lives of more than 115 million workers and families globally. Learn more at SHRM.org and on Twitter @SHRM.

Library of Congress Cataloging-in-Publication Data
Names: Society for Human Resource Management (U.S.), issuing body.
Title: Ace your SHRM certification exam: the official SHRM study guide for the SHRM-CP
    and SHRM-SCP exams / Society for Human Resource Management.
Description: Second edition. | Alexandria, Virginia : Society for Human Resource
    Management, [2022] | "Plus 40 SHRM-CP and SHRM-SCP practice items." | Includes
    bibliographical references and index.
Identifiers: LCCN 2021043827 (print) | LCCN 2021043828 (ebook) | ISBN 9781586441883
    (paperback) | ISBN 9781586442095 (pdf) | ISBN 9781586442279 (epub) | ISBN
    9781586444174 (mobi)
Subjects: LCSH: Personnel management--Examinations--Study guides. | Personnel management--Examinations, questions, etc. | Personnel departments--Employees--Certification.
Classification: LCC HF5549.15 .A34 2022 (print) | LCC HF5549.15 (ebook) | DDC
    658.30076--dc23

All product names, logos, and brands are property of their respective owners in the United States and/or other countries. All company, product, and service names used on this website are for identification purposes only.

SHRM®, SHRM-CP®, SHRM-SCP®, Learning System®, SHRM BASK™, and the "SHRM" logo are registered trademarks of SHRM.

Published in the United States of America   SECOND EDITION

PB Printing   10 9 8 7 6 5 4 3 2 1   SHRMStore SKU: 61.11513

Contents

PART 4

Exam Day

APPENDICES

Foreword

Congratulations! You're taking a big step toward moving ahead in your career as an HR professional. Choosing to follow an HR career path requires an interest in and dedication to lifelong learning.

Passing one of the SHRM certification exams bears witness to your dedication to the field of HR, your mastery of HR knowledge, and your ability to use what you know to behave competently in the workplace as an HR leader. Once you earn the SHRM-CP® or SHRM-SCP® credential, recertifying every three years becomes the next critical step toward your continued learning, growth, and competence as an HR professional.

SHRM hopes you will embrace certification as a critical step in a lifelong commitment to knowing, doing, learning, and growing as an HR professional. Your commitment to your own growth and development helps you create a better workplace and a better world. To help you succeed, SHRM created this study guide. This book will help you understand what SHRM recommends you learn and do to increase your chances of doing well on the exam. Preparing for a test is much like planning a vacation or business trip—the better the plan, the better able you will be to execute that plan and the more pleasant the entire experience will be.

In this book, we provide tools to guide you on your journey toward success on the SHRM-CP or SHRM-SCP certification exam. We recommend you leverage these resources to succeed. This study guide

» Provides an easy-to-use guide to help demystify the SHRM certification exams, with expert tips for understanding the material, studying, practicing, and reducing pretest anxiety so you can do your best on the exam;

» Covers everything you need to know about the exams, including development, content, structure, eligibility, administration, scoring, results, learning resources, and more;

» Features interviews with experts and tips from real test-takers on preparing for the exam and reducing test anxiety;

» Shows how to create a study plan based on your individual learning style and proven strategies for effective studying;

» Highlights how to practice taking the exam and how to best use the included forty-question practice test;

» Includes ready-to-use tools, templates, and worksheets to guide study and practice plans; and

» Details learning and study resources, including a guide to the terms and acronyms commonly used on the exam.

We also include special features that help you focus, organize, and plan your study time before taking the exam. These include

» Quotes, stories, and advice from former test takers;

» Key point summaries, infographics, and additional information highlighted for quick reference;

» Activities, including self-assessments and reflection tools; and

» Examples to illustrate core concepts.

Our hope is to prepare you to take the exam feeling confident that you have given yourself the best possible chance of passing.

We look forward to becoming and remaining your career partner, and we welcome the opportunity to support you as you learn, grow, know, and contribute to your workplace, develop as a professional, and advance the HR profession through those contributions. With SHRM Certification as the next step on your journey, we wish you success on the exam.

Best of luck in your professional development endeavors, and happy studying!

—Alexander Alonso, PhD, SHRM-SCP
Chief Knowledge Officer, Knowledge
Development & Certification
Society for Human Resource Management,
Alexandria, Virginia

Introduction

*"The only person you are destined to become
is the person you decide to be."*

—Ralph Waldo Emerson

The SHRM-CP and SHRM-SCP are the first-ever behavioral competency-based certifications for HR generalists, setting a new global standard in certification for the HR profession. By achieving and maintaining SHRM certification, you are making a commitment to lifelong learning about human resources.

Human resource (HR) professionals have increasingly used the term competency in recent years to describe a complex set of interrelated skills, knowledge, and abilities that are often associated with success in a specific job. This reflects the fact that acquisition of specific knowledge and experience before performing certain tasks does not necessarily produce the desired performance.

Success appears to require characteristics that may be harder to identify and measure, but nonetheless must be measured and reported for hiring managers to make the most effective decisions. Competencies—measurable or observable knowledge, skills, abilities, and other characteristics critical to successful job performance—fill this gap. Competency frameworks provide structure around those competencies for job success.

SHRM, the Society for Human Resource Management, set a goal of raising the caliber of the human resources profession. To do this, SHRM realized that the profession had to apply the principles of competencies and competency frameworks to its occupation. HR needed to identify what competencies were associated with effective, high-performing HR professionals. SHRM conducted this research with HR professionals in thirty-three countries. More than thirty-two thousand HR professionals participated in the development and validation of the eventual competency model.

SHRM's competency model reflects the breadth of HR's successful practice with various constituents, including HR's engaging

» With the organization vertically, from senior management to new hires;

» Across all divisions and functions of the organization horizontally;

> » With external stakeholders as well as internal customers; and

> » With groups, including entire workforces or individuals.

To succeed in this broad role, an HR professional must possess and demonstrate the nine competencies described in the SHRM Body of Applied Skills and Knowledge™ (SHRM BASK™): Leadership & Navigation; Ethical Practice; Diversity, Equity, & Inclusion; Relationship Management; Communication; Global Mindset; Business Acumen; Consultation; Analytical Aptitude; and HR Expertise (HR Knowledge).

HR Expertise, the technical competency, is the ability to apply HR principles and practices to the success of the organization. It is thoroughly defined in the fourteen functional areas of the SHRM BASK.

Why Take the Certification Exam?

HR professionals who have earned certification say that it enhances their credibility, helps them stay competitive in the job market, increases their confidence, and helps them keep up with developments in the HR field.

Each year, we survey thousands of former test takers to learn what role certification plays in their career development. Here's what we've found:

> » SHRM-certified professionals are more focused on continuous improvement for themselves and their organizations.

> » SHRM-certified professionals are more employable, are more likely to be promoted, and make more money.

> » SHRM-certified professionals have a more relevant skill set, are more productive, and demonstrate more leadership potential.

> » SHRM-certified professionals feel more satisfied with their careers.

> » SHRM-certified professionals benefit from ties to a supportive professional community.

Why This Book?

We wrote this book to share what we've learned from successful test takers about what worked when they prepared for and took a SHRM certification exam, including:

» Their insights on what it was like to prepare for a challenging exam,

» What they discovered about how their HR experience helped them succeed,

» How they created and stuck to a workable study plan and schedule so they would be ready on test day,

» How they managed any feelings of nervousness or anxiety they experienced,

» What test-taking strategies they used to help them answer the exam questions.

How the Book Is Organized

In Part 1, you'll find an overview of SHRM certification and the SHRM-CP and SHRM-SCP exams; an overview of the SHRM BASK; guidance for deciding which test to take and then determining whether you are eligible to take the exam level you chose; and an explanation of how the exams are created, administered, and scored.

Part 2 includes an exploration of learning styles so you can discover how you learn best, proven strategies for studying effectively, and guidance for creating a study plan that makes the most of your study time.

Part 3 covers the best practices for successful test taking that will help you draw on your HR experience and what you learn from studying to answer the questions on the exam, as well as strategies for reducing test anxiety and procrastination.

Part 4 gives you a preview of what to expect on test day, including information about taking the exam in a Prometric test center or via remote proctoring, as well as what happens after you take an exam.

The appendices contain helpful documents to support your learning journey, including a forty-question practice test and answer key, a glossary of terms, an acronym list used on the SHRM certification exams, and much more.

How to Use This Book

There are a variety of ways to prepare for the SHRM certification exams. This study guide is designed to supplement the preparation methods that are the best fit for you.

You can study on your own, using this book as a guide. You can participate in a structured learning program: SHRM offers a comprehensive certification preparation resource, the SHRM Learning System®, in a variety of formats—self-study and virtual or in-person seminars—and through partner universities that are authorized to teach the SHRM Learning System content. You can join with other certification candidates to form a study group, many of which form organically through SHRM chapters.

Whichever method or methods you choose, a key part of your preparation will be thinking through the types of situations, challenges, problems, and opportunities you encounter in your day-to-day HR work.

How This Book Was Developed

This book is a collaborative effort among the SHRM staff in various divisions, along with expert assistance from a seasoned book writer and editor and SHRM-certified subject matter experts. There are many moving parts in test development and administration, so each internal expert contributed their piece of the puzzle to provide you with a complete picture of the exam, the test-day experience, and what it takes to prepare. Our goal is to provide as much helpful information in one source as possible and to dispel myths about the SHRM certification exams so that you can be ready for success on test day.

The first edition of this book was published in 2019. To reflect the ever-changing nature of the exam, SHRM revised and expanded the book in this second edition. A few of the major changes include the following:

» Updating the content to reflect the changes in the 2022 SHRM BASK.

» Adding information about the option to test via live remote proctoring and how to decide whether it's the best option for you.

» Revising the information about the structure of the exam, including the total testing time and number of exam questions.

» Adding a new chapter about the most and least effective strategies for reasoning through an item, with examples (see Chapter 9).

» Doubling the number of questions in the practice test to 40 items (see Appendix 2).

A Word about What This Book Is NOT

This book is not a deep dive into the SHRM BASK. For success on the certification exam, we encourage you to review the SHRM BASK carefully and use it to map out your study plan. Here's why:

» The SHRM BASK represents the results from a comprehensive practice analysis—it is detailed and comprehensive because its contents represent the entirety of the practice of HR as validated through empirical research.

» The SHRM BASK is a roadmap to every topic that is considered "fair game" for exam questions. It covers hundreds of topics, and we suggest a focused review to augment and inform your study plan. Keep in mind that there are 134 questions on the exam compared with hundreds if not thousands of concepts presented in the SHRM BASK.

» As you review the SHRM BASK, use the content to differentiate between the areas you have mastered and those you need to learn more about. Identifying what you do and do not know about the topics covered in the SHRM BASK will help you craft a study plan and strategy that works best for you. We'll talk about this further in Part 2.

Let's get started!

 ONLINE

Access the interactive SHRM Body of Applied Skills and Knowledge (SHRM BASK) here:

https://www.shrm.org/certification/about
/BodyofAppliedSkillsandKnowledge/Pages
/Download-SHRM-BASK.aspx

Acknowledgments

This resource was made possible by the thoughtful and generous advice, guidance, and input of many smart and talented subject matter experts, especially the following:

Alexander Alonso, PhD, SHRM-SCP, Chief Knowledge Officer, SHRM

Nancy Woolever, MAIS, SHRM-SCP, Vice President, Certification, SHRM

Selina Russ, Senior Specialist, Form Development, SHRM

Mark Smith, PhD, Director, HR Thought Leadership Research, SHRM

Ashley Silver, SHRM-CP, Test Development Specialist, SHRM

Nathan Forrester, Certification Research Analyst, SHRM

Nicholas Schacht, SHRM-SCP, Chief Global Development Officer, SHRM

Charles Glover, Manager, Exam Development & Accreditation, SHRM

Scott Oppler, PhD, Senior Technical Advisor, Human Resource Research Organization (HumRRO)

Jeanne Morris, Vice President, Education, SHRM

Susie Davis, Director, Digital Education, SHRM

Eddice L. Douglas, SHRM-CP, Specialist, Certification Educational Products, SHRM

Patricia Byrd, Director, Certification Relations, SHRM

Janis Fisher Chan, Lead Writer and Developmental Editor, first edition

We also gratefully acknowledge the scores of SHRM members, test takers, and exam candidates who volunteered to share their stories and offer tips for this book.

Part 1

About the SHRM-CP and SHRM-SCP Certification Exams

"Without continual growth and progress, such words as improvement, achievement, and success have no meaning."

–Benjamin Franklin

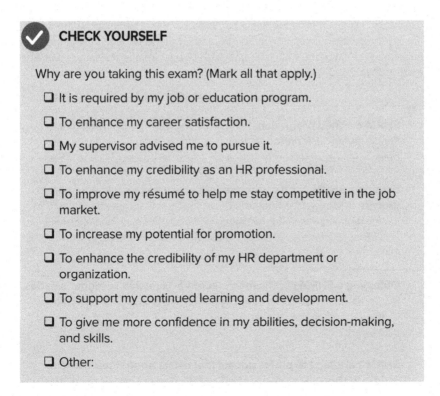

CHECK YOURSELF

Why are you taking this exam? (Mark all that apply.)

- ❑ It is required by my job or education program.
- ❑ To enhance my career satisfaction.
- ❑ My supervisor advised me to pursue it.
- ❑ To enhance my credibility as an HR professional.
- ❑ To improve my résumé to help me stay competitive in the job market.
- ❑ To increase my potential for promotion.
- ❑ To enhance the credibility of my HR department or organization.
- ❑ To support my continued learning and development.
- ❑ To give me more confidence in my abilities, decision-making, and skills.
- ❑ Other:

Identify Your Reasons for Pursuing Certification

Candidates who take the SHRM-CP and SHRM-SCP exams take them for many different reasons. It is important to think about why *you* are taking this exam because it will help you focus on achieving your goal to become SHRM-certified.

At some point during your certification study, your motivation will likely drop. You'll want to skip your study group, take a break from your flash cards for a few days, or give up on taking the exam altogether.

When that happens, revisit this page. Think about the specific reasons why you decided to start this journey and how you and your career will benefit from a SHRM credential. Then recommit to making it happen.

Career Benefits of SHRM Certification

Earning a SHRM-CP or SHRM-SCP certification has become increasingly valuable to HR professionals. Every HR professional who takes one of the exams has personal reasons for seeking certification, but the benefits of a SHRM certification are significant and widespread, as shown in a large study of HR professionals in 2020–2021.

» **SHRM-certified professionals have strong workplace credibility.**
SHRM-certified HR professionals are significantly more likely to report being well respected among their professional colleagues and peers.

» **Earning a SHRM certification credential can help you in your career growth.** Seventy-seven percent of HR professionals agreed that SHRM certification increases the likelihood of landing a job in the field of HR, and 88 percent agree it increases the likelihood of obtaining a promotion in the field of HR.

» **Obtaining a SHRM certification credential is related to higher salaries.**
HR professionals who pass the SHRM-CP and SHRM-SCP certification exams report salaries that are 14–15 percent higher than those who fail the exams.

» **SHRM-certified HR professionals feel better about their careers.**
SHRM-certified HR professionals have 30 percent higher commitment

to the profession of HR and 17 percent greater likelihood of pride in the quality of work they have produced. They also report high career satisfaction at a significantly higher rate (+22 percent) than non-certified professionals.

» **SHRM-certified professionals have fewer concerns about job security.** Only 4 percent of SHRM-certified HR professionals reported being "very concerned" about their job security, while 22 percent of noncertified HR professionals reported feeling this way.

Organizational Benefit from SHRM Certification

HR professionals are not the only beneficiaries of a SHRM-CP or SHRM-SCP certification. SHRM research shows that the HR department and the entire organization can gain tangible and valuable advantages too. Once you set your certification goal, use these four points to demonstrate why your manager and organization should support your efforts to prepare for and attain certification.

When studying the various components of an HR professional's career, SHRM research conducted in 2021 showed there are four top ways your organization will benefit from you earning your SHRM-CP or your SHRM-SCP certification:

» **Your HR knowledge will be current and relevant.** SHRM-certified HR professionals are 60 percent more likely to agree they have current and up-to-date information on HR best practices. You will have access to extensive resources through SHRM: SHRM news articles, toolkits, and other resources on the shrm.org website that you can apply to your organization. Attaining and maintain your credential means you will be ready to take on more challenging responsibilities.

» **You will continue to learn practical skills that will positively impact your job.** SHRM-certified professionals complete almost twice as many learning and development activities per year as noncertified professionals. After becoming certified, you will engage in activities like attending conferences, mentoring and coaching, networking, and reading books and articles—so the learning never stops. You will be applying concepts, using judgment, and understanding HR's best practices for both day-to-day and unexpected scenarios. Seventy-two percent of all HR professionals agree SHRM certification helps in maintaining compliance with the law as well.

» **You will be better prepared for business challenges.** Growing the influence of HR leaders through certification is a worthwhile investment that also improves your organization's reputation as one that takes HR seriously. Just as a certified project management professional (PMP) is trusted to know how to successfully lead projects and people, you will earn the same type of trust with your SHRM-CP or SHRM-SCP credential. The decisions you make will positively affect your organization. In fact, 64 percent of SHRM-certified HR professionals report their decisions impacted their organization versus 46 percent of noncertified HR professionals.

» **Your knowledge and skills will be globally applicable and universally recognized.** Earning a SHRM credential will give you the confidence and ability to use the knowledge and skills you have acquired anywhere in your organization, now and in the future. The SHRM BASK is the foundation of your SHRM credential. SHRM regularly conducts global research to validate and update the SHRM BASK so it remains relevant and reflects the future of HR. SHRM research shows that SHRM-certified HR professionals report levels of respect from their professional colleagues and peers at a higher rate than noncertified counterparts—80 percent of HR professionals believe SHRM Certification adds to the overall credibility of an HR department.

Chapter 1

The Exams and What They Test

An Overview of the SHRM Body of Applied Skills and Knowledge (SHRM BASK), the Two Exams, and Accreditation

"Live as if you were to die tomorrow. Learn as if you were to live forever."

–Mahatma Gandhi

The SHRM certification exams test your capabilities in both aspects of HR practice—applied skills and knowledge—that are required for effective job performance. The exams are based upon the core set of applied skills and knowledge outlined in the SHRM BASK. SHRM certification exams are accredited by the Buros Center for Testing at University of Nebraska–Lincoln.

A product of rigorous research involving thousands of HR professionals, the SHRM BASK identifies nine key behavioral competencies and fourteen HR functional areas that are critical to the success of any HR professional. The SHRM BASK will be your study outline as you prepare for your exam (see Figure 1.1).

 ONLINE
Download the SHRM Body of Applied Skills and Knowledge (SHRM BASK)

https://www.shrm.org/certification/about
/BodyofAppliedSkillsandKnowledge/Pages
/Download-SHRM-BASK.aspx

Figure 1.1. Know Your SHRM BASK!

For Examinees Who Test Outside of the United States

The SHRM BASK includes one functional area that covers US employment laws and regulations. However, questions in this functional area do not appear on exams for examinees who reside *and* take an exam outside of the United States. If you reside and take your exam outside of the United States, you will still have the same number of scored and nonscored items on your exam; however, all questions from the US Employment Law and Regulations functional area will be removed and replaced with items from other sections of the SHRM BASK that are globally applicable. There are no changes to the questions on the exams that fall under the remaining nine behavioral competencies and thirteen functional areas.

SNAPSHOP
What Accreditation Is and Why It Matters

Accreditation for a credentialing program provides important corroboration of the program's quality and rigor as determined by an independent, qualified third party against a set of established standard of quality measured by the testing industry. The SHRM-CP and SHRM-SCP are accredited by the Buros Center for Testing at the University of Nebraska—Lincoln.

The Buros Center evaluates the psychometric quality of credentialing testing programs like SHRM's testing program. The center conducts a general audit of the program's processes and procedures along with a yearly, focused evaluation of specific testing windows within the program. SHRM participates in both types of accreditation audit—the periodic general audit and the annual, focused testing-year evaluation.

Buros reviews SHRM's policies and procedures to ensure the SHRM-CP and SHRM-SCP maintain the required quality standards that apply to testing programs. Its review is based on the extent to which SHRM's testing program demonstrates that it meets the Buros Standards for Accreditation of Testing Programs. At the end of each audit phase, Buros provides evidence that the SHRM-CP and SHRM-SCP exams adhere to those standards, along with ways in which the policies or procedures could be modified or improved to meet or address emerging expectations of the professional community.

The Buros Standards are periodically updated to reflect current guidelines from the testing community. In particular, the Center's Standards are highly consistent with the 2014 Standards for Educational and Psychological Testing, jointly published by the American Educational Research Association (AERA), the American Psychological Association (APA), and the National Council on Measurement in Education (NCME). The Buros National Advisory Council unanimously approved its revised standards in June 2017. SHRM provides information annually to maintain its accreditation for the SHRM-CP and SHRM-SCP certifications.

Recognized by HR Employers

The fastest-growing program in the HR certification community. More than 30,500 applicants sought SHRM certification in 2020, and more than half of job postings listed SHRM credential holders as preferred applicants.

Meets the Highest Standards

The SHRM-CP and SHRM-SCP exams are accredited by the Buros Center for Testing, the global leader in evaluating the psychometric quality of examinations. They are an independent body that reviews SHRM policies and procedures to ensure a standard of quality as measured by testing industry professionals.

Fueled by HR Competencies

SHRM certification is powered by the SHRM BASK™, which was developed and validated by more than forty thousand HR professionals. Nine out of ten non-HR business executives view competencies as important for overall HR department success.

Engineered by Experts

Each year, approximately 1,000 subject matter experts from around the world come together over the course of twenty-eight workshops to develop new items for SHRM certification exams. SHRM certification exam development is led by top-notch, professionally trained exam development experts with an average of thirty years of experience.

Raises the Global Standards

SHRM certification has worldwide reach with credential-holders in 105 countries. SHRM's Certification Commission ensures the quality and impartiality of the SHRM certification program.

Built with Your Future in Mind

SHRM's competency-based certification was designed to transport you across 100 percent of your HR career. With more than 110,000 educational programs and a network of over 3,100+ providers, SHRM supports you through recertification and lifelong professional development in an ever-changing industry.

Figure 1.2. Six Things You Should Know About SHRM Certification

TABLE 1.1. SHRM-CP and SHRM-SCP Eligibility

SHRM Certified Professional (SHRM-CP)

- The SHRM-CP certification is for individuals who perform general HR/HR-related duties or for those pursuing a career in Human Resource Management.
- Candidates for the SHRM-CP certification are not required to hold an HR title and do not need a degree or previous HR experience to apply; however, a basic working knowledge of HR practices and principles is recommended.
- The SHRM-CP exam is designed to assess the competency level of those who engage in HR work at the operational level. Work at this level includes duties such as implementing HR policies, supporting day-to-day HR functions, or serving as an HR point of contact for staff and stakeholders.
- Refer to the SHRM BASK for detailed information on proficiency standards for this credential (i.e., Proficiency Indicators for All HR Professionals).

SHRM Senior Certified Professional (SHRM-SCP)

- The SHRM-SCP certification is for individuals who have a work history of at least three years performing strategic level HR/HR-related duties or for SHRM-CP credential holders who have held the credential for at least three years and are working in, or are in the process of transitioning to, a strategic level role.
- Candidates for the SHRM-SCP certification are not required to hold an HR title and do not need a degree to apply.
- The SHRM-SCP exam is designed to assess the competency level of those who engage in HR work at the strategic level. Work at this level includes duties such as developing HR policies and procedures, overseeing the execution of integrated HR operations, directing an entire HR enterprise, or leading the alignment of HR strategies to organizational goals.
- Applicants must be able to demonstrate that they devoted at least one thousand hours per calendar year (Jan.–Dec.) to strategic level HR/HR-related work. More than one thousand hours in a calendar year does not equate to more than one year of experience.
- Part-time work qualifies as long as the one-thousand-hour per calendar year standard is met.
- Experience may be either salaried or hourly.
- Individuals who are HR consultants may demonstrate qualifying experience through the HR/HR-related duties they perform for their clients. Contracted hours must meet the one-thousand-hour standard.
- Refer to the SHRM BASK for detailed information on proficiency standards for this credential (i.e., Proficiency Indicators for All HR Professionals and for Advanced HR Professionals).

Two Certification Exams and Eligibility

SHRM offers two levels of certification: the SHRM-CP and the SHRM-SCP. You should choose the exam level that best matches your job duties and then cross-check the eligibility table (Table 1.1) to determine whether you meet the specific eligibility requirements for the exam level you selected.

» The **SHRM-CP** is designed for HR professionals who primarily work (or will work) in an operational role, such as implementing policies, serving as the HR point of contact, and performing day-to-day HR functions.

» The **SHRM-SCP** is designed for HR professionals who primarily work in a strategic role, such as developing policies and strategies, overseeing the execution of integrated HR operations, directing the entire HR enterprise, and leading the alignment of HR strategies to organizational goal.

Which exam you take depends on which certification aligns most closely with your job responsibilities and level of experience and whether you meet the specific eligibility requirements.

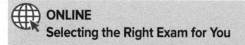 **ONLINE**
Selecting the Right Exam for You

Not sure which exam to take? Use the interactive wizard on the Certification website to help you determine which credential is right for you. After answering a series of questions about your career level, education, and types of experience, you will receive a recommendation about which certification to pursue. To use the wizard, go to the following webpage and scroll down to the large yellow banner that says, "Which Credential Is Right for You?"

https://www.shrm.org/certification/apply/eligibility-criteria/Pages/which-exam-to-take.aspx

If you are still not sure which SHRM certification exam to take even after reviewing the descriptions of the exams and the online wizard, we recommend that you start with the SHRM-CP and then work to pass the SHRM-SCP later in your career.

How to Apply

SHRM offers both certification exams during two testing windows every year. The first window is from May 1 to July 15, and the second window is from December 1 to February 15. Examinees can choose to take the exam in person at one of more than 500 Prometric testing centers across more than 85 countries with up to 6,000 seats daily, or they can choose to take it via live remote proctor.

Once you have decided which exam to take, register to take the exam on the SHRM website anytime between the Applications Accepted Starting Date and the Standard Application Deadline. Examinees who apply by the Early-Bird Application Deadline and/or who are SHRM members receive a reduced exam fee. Note that exam applications apply for specific testing windows; once you have applied, transfers to the following testing windows are possible but involve a separate transfer fee.

To register, you will:

1. Create a user account.

2. Select which level exam you want to take.

3. Complete the application form and sign the SHRM Certification Candidate Agreement.

4. Pay the registration fee.

5. Once you receive your Authorization-to-Test (ATT) letter, schedule your exam. Your ATT letter will outline several ways to schedule.

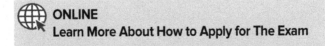

ONLINE
Learn More About How to Apply for The Exam

https://www.shrm.org/certification/apply/Pages
/applicationprocess.aspx

Chapter 2

Exam Structure and Question Types

"In failing to prepare, you are preparing to fail."

—Benjamin Franklin

An important part of preparing yourself for the test is knowing what kinds of questions you will be asked and how the test is structured and administered.

The structure and administration of the SHRM-CP and SHRM-SCP exams are nearly identical. They have the same number of questions, the same question structure, and the same amount of exam time. Because of this similarity between exams, most of the advice provided in this book will be relevant to both exams. The largest difference is in the types of questions asked— the SHRM-CP focuses on the operational level, while the SHRM-SCP is more focused on strategy and effectively managing an HR department.

Recall that the SHRM BASK is based on a global practice analysis of the HR profession and provides the basis for developing the SHRM certification exams. The test blueprint is derived from the SHRM BASK. It provides the framework that specifies how many questions are included on each exam from each of the SHRM BASK's nine behavioral competencies and fourteen HR knowledge areas (or thirteen HR knowledge areas for candidates taking the exams outside of the United States, as explained in Chapter 1).

Two item types comprise the SHRM certification exams: knowledge items (KIs) and situational judgment items (SJIs).

QUICK TIP

To see examples of real, previously administered exam questions, check out the practice test in Appendix 2. It contains KIs and SJIs that appeared on SHRM certification tests in the recent years and provides a realistic preview of what you can expect operational exam questions to look like in format, structure, and content. Keep in mind that none of the items on this or any practice test will appear on the operational exam you take on test day.

Knowledge Items

Knowledge items are **stand-alone multiple-choice items**, and each tests a single piece of knowledge or application of knowledge. KIs test your knowledge of key concepts; terms in the HR field and your ability to apply them by demonstrating ability to recall knowledge; and understanding, solving problems, and predicting outcomes by applying knowledge using the four levels in the depth of knowledge framework. Knowledge items have only one, irrefutably correct response option called the *key*. Each knowledge item is linked to a specific source and has a rationale that explains why the key is the only correct answer and the three other response options are incorrect.

Knowledge items are further divided into two types.

» HR-specific knowledge items (KIs) cover key concept topics associated with the fourteen HR functional areas defined in the SHRM BASK.

» Foundational knowledge items (FKIs) cover the key concepts that are considered foundational to each of the nine behavioral competencies.

There are a total of eighty knowledge items on the SHRM exams, including both KIs and FKIs. You receive credit for selecting the key, or the correct answer. Points are not deducted for incorrect responses or for guesses.

Each knowledge item is classified according to the depth of knowledge, or level of understanding or application, required to answer it. There are four levels in the depth of knowledge framework: (1) recall, (2) understanding, (3) problem-solving, and (4) critical evaluation. Level 1 recall questions make up 15 to 20 percent of the knowledge items on the SHRM certification exams, while higher level questions make up the remaining 80 to 85 percent of knowledge items. Both KIs and FKIs include items written across the four levels in the depth of knowledge framework.

Basic Level: "Recall" Questions

Recall questions represent the base of the framework, reflecting the surface of cognitive complexity. They serve an important purpose by requiring test takers to access and recite information stored in their brains.

Recall questions may ask the test taker to define a specific term, or they may supply a definition and ask the test taker to identify the term being defined.

Example of a recall question and answer that could appear on a SHRM exam:

> **Q:** What change management model follows the pattern of "unfreeze, change, refreeze"?
>
> **A:** Lewin's Model

Next Level: "Understanding" Questions

The more rigorous *understanding* questions act as a shovel to break through the Level 1 recall surface. They require test takers to comprehend information, compare two things, translate by applying knowledge, or interpret a concept to apply it. In other words, they assess one's ability to recognize how HR concepts and terms manifest themselves in the workplace.

Understanding questions are designed to ensure that candidates who pass the exam are both knowledgeable and possess the skills and abilities required to be a competent HR professional.

Example of an understanding question and answer that mirrors the operational exam content and structure:

> **Q:** During a board meeting, a leader at a technology company describes a potential crisis that threatens the company's ability to operate. This action implements which step in Kotter's eight-step change management model?
>
> **A:** Creating a sense of urgency

To answer this question, the test taker needs to remember all the steps in Kotter's model and how to apply them properly.

High Level: "Problem-Solving" Questions

Problem-Solving questions require test takers to apply their knowledge to develop a solution to a problem, which is something HR professionals do every day. To select the correct answer, one must draw on one's knowledge and understanding of many different concepts and strategies, which is more cognitively demanding than the recall of information.

Example of a problem-solving question and answer that mirrors the operational exam content and structure:

> **Q:** After a recent layoff, the CEO announces plans to restructure the organization. Which action should leadership take first to help hesitant employees adjust to the changes?
>
> **A:** Identify strong senior sponsorship for the change.

The problem presented in this question is the employees' hesitation. To answer, the test taker needs to identify the action that will most effectively help them overcome it.

Highest Level: "Critical Evaluation" Questions

Critical Evaluation questions, which ask test takers to analyze information to predict an outcome, are the most challenging. A competent HR professional uses the ability to predict outcomes to guide business strategy and execution.

Example of a critical evaluation question that mirrors the operational exam content and structure:

> **Q:** During a change management initiative, which outcome is most likely to happen if an organization focuses only on the bottom line?
>
> **A:** The impacts of the change to the individuals currently working in the organization are overlooked.

Here, the test taker must have knowledge of change management initiatives and how organizations choose to implement them. Using that knowledge, the HR professional should recommend ways to minimize any negative effects.

Situational Judgment Items

In comparison, situational judgment items (SJIs) present realistic situations that are likely to occur in workplaces throughout the world and are similar to what many HR professionals have likely experienced during their careers. Based on the scenario presented, SJIs ask test takers to consider the problem presented in the question within the context of the situation, and then select the *best course of action to take.*

Like knowledge items, each SJI has four response options from which to choose. Unlike knowledge items, SJIs test decision-making and judgment skills—not application of knowledge. Instead, they allow you to use what you know to show you know how to make competent decisions and judgments. Therefore, the response options range from most effective to least effective course of action. It is important to note that SJIs do not test your company's approach, your own approach, or your industry's approach. They test what competent behavior looks like in action as defined by the proficiency standards (called proficiency indicators) in the SHRM BASK for each of the nine behavioral competencies.

There are fifty-four SJIs on the SHRM exams.

HR professionals from many countries around the world provide the "raw materials" for situational judgment items, which are critical incidents drawn from real-life situations that are likely to be common situations that occur in workplaces in every country across the world. HR professionals also provide multiple courses of action to take in the situation, with possible actions ranging from very effective to very ineffective. Figure 2.1 depicts the entire SJI development process.

 QUICK TIP

It may be helpful to streamline your thinking about SJIs to remove some of the mystery that accompanies this item type. Think about SJIs this way: they require you to do nothing different than what you do *every day* at work: something happens, you need to figure out everything occurring in the situation, you need to decide what is the best thing to do in this situation, then you take action by implementing that best course of action.

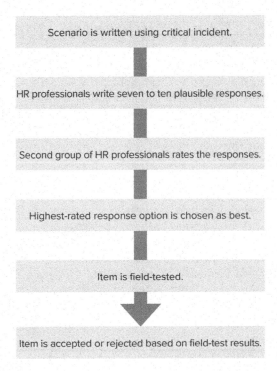

Figure 2.1. How Situational Judgment Items (SJIs) are Created

How SHRM Determines the Most Effective or Best Response to an SJI

Scoring panels, which are composed of seasoned SHRM-certified HR professionals, rate the various responses to identify the "best" or "most effective" response as the key. These experts rate more than four response options; in general, these teams review eight to ten possible responses and assign to each possible response option a numeric equivalent ranging from most effective to least effective. Statistical analysis of effectiveness ratings then determines the key. Because the best answer is based on expert judgments, no rationale exists other than that the key is selected based on the aggregated judgments of expert panelists.

The examinee must choose the most effective course of action based on the definition of best practice—and the definition of best practice appears in the SHRM BASK content. Consider that more than one of the possible strategies might be effective, but only one will be the best or most effective course of action (also called the key) based on the situation and as decided by the panel

SNAPSHOP
Just How Do You Test Behavior?

SHRM's certification exams use situational judgment items (SJIs) to assess abilities that are defined in the nine behavioral competencies included in the SHRM BASK. For the HR profession, behaving competently is inextricably linked to HR knowledge. Thus, SJIs allow certification candidates to use what they know to demonstrate how to behave competently in a given situation.

For SHRM-CP and SHRM-SCP test takers, an effective way to think about SJIs is to reflect on what occurs in the workplace day-in and day-out. That means thinking about how your behavior affects the outcome of any given situation at work—whether it is solving an employee relations issue, leading a strategic initiative to determine the details of a future-focused workforce development plan, or creating a business continuity plan to safeguard the organization from risk.

These types of situations require you as an HR professional to use what you know and know how to do to perform competently (behavior), as defined in the nine behavioral competencies outlined in the SHRM BASK. Different situations require different behaviors, for example, leading ethically, communicating, consulting, or managing relationships effectively. This is why SJIs on the exam ask you to select the most effective course of action from the four possible response options.

This is very similar in concept to riding a bicycle or driving an automobile: you must know the "rules of the road," but you also need to know how to competently operate the bicycle or automobile.

of SHRM-certified HR professionals. Panelists use the proficiency indicators in the SHRM BASK for each of the nine behavioral competencies when rating the effectiveness of each response on the scale from most effective to least effective. Therefore, it is important to be well-acquainted with the proficiency indicators for the nine behavioral competencies. Also note that because SJIs test judgment and decision-making instead of application of knowledge, SJIs questions are not written using the four levels in the depth of knowledge framework.

You will need to use what you know and things you know how to do in order to behave competently by making a good decision, but SJIs do not test knowledge. They test ability to use knowledge as a foundation for performing competently as defined by the proficiency indicators.

The Importance of Field-Testing KIs and SJIs

Before a KI or an SJI can be part of the scored, operational test-item set, each one must first be subjected to field testing. *Field test items*, including both KIs and SJIs, are used to determine the psychometric properties of an item, such as item difficulty and ability to differentiate between test takers. This information is used to help gauge the overall quality of an item to determine its eligibility to become a scored item on a future SHRM-CP or SHRM-SCP exam. Taken as a group, responses to field test questions serve two purposes. First, they help to identify items that are possible additions to future exams. Second, they support growth of the certification program by assessing item quality. These factors determine the field test item's eligibility to be retained in the item bank and to be placed on a future test form. If a field test item is viable, as determined by a required set of standards, only then does the item move from "field test" status to "operational" status.

Currently, there are 24 field test questions out of the 134 total items on each exam. Field test items are randomly mixed with other items and are not scored. Only the 110 operational set of KIs and SJIs are scored and contribute to a pass/fail decision.

Both KIs and SJIs undergo field-testing, meaning each item is initially included as a nonscored item on an exam to determine its readiness to become a scored test item. If an item meets quality standards after it is field-tested, it becomes eligible for scoring as part of a future operational item pool. If it does not meet quality standards, the item is not eligible to become a scored item or used on a future test form.

SHRM's Item-Writing Methodology

Each year, approximately 1,000 SHRM-certified HR subject matter experts from around the world come together over the course of twenty-eight workshops—including fourteen SHRM-CP workshops and fourteen SHRM-SCP workshops—to develop and refine new items for SHRM certification exams.

SHRM certification exam development is led by top-notch, professionally trained exam development experts who guide the subject matter experts through the process of drafting exam items. After exam items are drafted, the items go through several rounds of review to validate that the content and key is correct, the item is applicable to the field of HR, and the item does not contain bias or cultural sensitivity issues.

SHRM requires its item writers to write questions in simple, clear language that is straightforward and easy to understand by professionals across the world. SHRM's intent is to provide you a wide variety of questions so you are able to show, through your answers on an exam, what you know and know how to do for KIs. For SJIs, the goal is to provide you a wide variety of questions so you are able to show that you can perform at a competent level using what you know and know how to do. Because of this, there are no "trick" questions on the SHRM certification exams.

Contrary to what is discussed frequently on social media, it is also important to understand there are no "SHRM" answers. As we've discussed, the test questions are written, edited, and reviewed by and the answers are selected by SHRM-certified HR professionals. The SHRM staff provides expertise in test development, not HR subject-matter expertise. Thus, SHRM relies on thousands of SHRM-certified subject matter experts to create the actual test content. This is why there is no "SHRM" answer.

 QUICK TIP

To see examples of real exam questions that were previously on a SHRM exam, check out the forty-question practice test in Appendix 2 or try a few online practice questions here: https://certpracticequestions.shrm.org/. Keep in mind that none of these practice questions—or any other practice questions that you take—will appear on the exam you take on test day.

SHRM-CP and SHRM-SCP Exam Structure

Both the SHRM-CP and SHRM-SCP certification exams consist of 134 questions. Each exam is broken into two equal halves, and each half contains 67 questions. Each half is divided into three sections: first, a section of 20 KIs and FKIs; then a section of 27 SJIs; and finally, another section of 20 KIs and FKIs (see Figure 2.2).

Examinees must complete the first half of an exam before moving on to the second half. Once an examinee begins the second half, the examinee cannot return to the first half to review questions or change answers.

Exam Timing

The total exam appointment time is four hours, which includes three hours and forty minutes of testing time for the exam itself. The exam time is broken down into:

Introduction (including the confidentiality reminder)—four minutes

Tutorial—eight minutes

Exam Half 1—Up to one hour and fifty minutes

Exam Half 2—Up to one hour and fifty minutes

Survey—six minutes

There are a few transition screens throughout the exam that account for the remaining minutes. Remember that you can take an unscheduled break of up to fifteen minutes. There is no scheduled break between the first and second sections, which means that you can take your break at any time. When you take your break, the exam clock will continue to run. See Chapter 11 for more information about how to strategically use your break time.

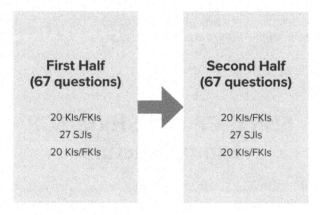

Figure 2.2. Exam Structure

Each section shows a countdown timer on the screen, so you can keep track of how much time you have left. Also, each section is separate and timed independently. Minutes do not roll over. For instance, if you spend less time in the tutorial, those extra minutes are not rolled over to the first exam half.

Exam Items by Content and Item Type

The distribution of items with respect to content and item type is essentially the same for both the SHRM-CP and SHRM-SCP exams. About half of the items on each exam are allocated across the three behavioral competency clusters, and the other half are allocated across the three HR knowledge domains. Approximately 40 percent of the items on each exam are situational judgment items, with the remainder being stand-alone items measuring either knowledge that is foundational to the behavioral competencies (10 percent) or HR-specific knowledge (50 percent).

Item Type

Situational Judgment (40%)	HR-Specific Knowledge (50%)
Foundational Knowledge (10%)	

Behavioral Competency Clusters

HR Knowledge Domains

Leadership (17%)	People (18%)
Business (16.5%)	Organization (18%)
Interpersonal (16.5%)	Workplace (14%)

Figure 2.3. Distribution of Exam Items by Content and Exam Type

How the Exams Are Administered

The SHRM-CP and SHRM-SCP exams are administered via computer-based testing. Examinees can take an exam either in-person at a highly secure Prometric testing center or virtually using live remote proctoring. *Live remote proctoring* means the testing session is monitored by a qualified proctor through audio-video and screen-share feed in real time.

Once your exam application has been accepted for a testing window, you will schedule your exam on the Prometric website or by calling Prometric directly. When scheduling your exam, you will decide whether to take your exam in-person at a testing center or via live remote proctoring.

Before you schedule your exam via remote proctoring, run the system readiness check to verify that your computer meets the minimum system requirements. In addition, think carefully about your needs and the testing experience that you think will work best for you. Consider why remote proctored testing might be a good option for you and why it might not be the best fit. For example, if your computer does not meet the minimum system requirements or you do not have access to a stable internet connection, live remote proctoring is not a good option for you. Use the following questions and answers as a start to guide your choice. You can also read about what to expect on exam day for each mode in Chapter 11.

 ONLINE

Complete Prometric's system readiness check to determine whether your operating system is compatible to install and run the ProProctor™ application so that you can take a remotely proctored exam: https://rpcandidate.prometric.com/

Why Might Remote Proctored Testing Be a Good Option for Me?

There are many reasons people choose to test remotely. One of these reasons might fit your circumstance:

» Testing in a familiar place helps ease some of your test anxiety issues.

» The nearest test center is farther away than you wish to travel.

» The convenience of testing anytime/anywhere gives you more control over your experience.

» There are no in-person seats available at the time you want to test.

Why Might Remote Proctored Testing NOT Be a Good Option for Me?

Remote proctored testing isn't for everyone. When you take a SHRM certification exam via remote proctoring, your home or office *becomes* the testing center. This means you are responsible for ensuring the security of your exam as well as providing the computer and internet connection to complete the exam. Here are some strong reasons why remote proctoring might *not* be the best option for you:

» You do not have access to a computer that meets Prometric's system requirements.

» You do not have a strong, stable internet connection.

» You do not have a quiet, private room (with a door that closes) at your home or office to take the exam.

» You want to have immediate access to an in-person test center administrator in case something goes wrong with your exam.

 ONLINE

Learn more about taking a SHRM-CP or
SHRM-SCP exam from Prometric by visiting
https://www.prometric.com/SHRM.

Chapter 3

Exam Scoring

SHRM uses a rigorous scoring process for certification exams, which includes third-party independent validation and verification. Passing scores are set using a best-practice that is commonly used procedure for high-stakes certification and licensing exams. This is known as setting the performance standard.

Your individual performance will be measured against the predetermined standard, not against that of other people taking the test. To maintain the integrity of the SHRM Certification Program, the SHRM Certification Commission evaluates the scoring standard recommendations and ensures the technical quality of all test-scoring practices.

After you have finished the test, the system calculates a Pass/Did Not Pass result, posts a statement on your screen, and emails the Pass/Did Not Pass result to the email address you used when scheduling your testing appointment. You will receive the official score report about two to three weeks after you take the test. The official score report will be posted to your SHRM Certification account in the certification portal.

How the Exams Are Scored

Many candidates ask SHRM how the SHRM-CP and SHRM-SCP certification examinations are scored, and how those scores are reported to examinees. The most frequently asked questions include:

» Why is 200 the passing score when the exam has 134 questions?

» Do I have to earn the maximum score to pass the exam?

» What is the number of questions I must answer correctly to pass the exam?

» What is the number of questions I must answer correctly in the SHRM Learning System to know if I will pass the exam?

First, let's talk about how SHRM sets the passing scores for the SHRM certification exams. SHRM employs best-practice procedures most commonly used for setting performance standards for certification and licensure exams. During a multiday evaluation process, a panel of experienced HR professionals evaluates the exam questions to determine how difficult they are for a candidate who is "just-qualified" or "minimally qualified" at the appropriate level: SHRM-CP (for those in operational roles) or SHRM-SCP (for those in strategic roles).

To keep the SHRM certification exams up-to-date and fair, during every testing window we add and remove questions. Before a new question is used, it is first pretested (also called field-testing) with real examinees. We do that by mixing 24 unscored field test questions into each exam. Examinees answer the field test questions, but answers to field test questions are not part of the pass decision. In other words, of the 134 questions on the exam that you answer, 110 are used to calculate your score; the 24 field test items do not count. Because there is no way for you to know which questions count toward your score and which do not, it is important to do your best on all test items.

After the field test items are pretested, SHRM analyzes each item's statistical quality. Only those questions that meet the performance standards become scored items on future exams. Each test form of 134 items changes every time an exam administration occurs.

Raw Scores and Scaled Scores

The SHRM-CP and SHRM-SCP exams have 134 questions, and 110 of them are used to calculate your score. After you take the test, you will have a *raw score* of 0–110 correctly selected keys; but the score we report to you is *on a scale* of 120–200, with "passing" set at 200—this is known as your *scaled score*.

It is a common and best practice in standardized testing to place the number of questions answered correctly on a scale (scaled score), rather than to simply report to the examinee the number of questions answered correctly (raw score). You may be familiar with this process if you have taken the SAT or ACT for college, the GRE for graduate school, or the GMAT for a master's degree in business administration. The scores for these exams range from 400–1600 for the SAT, 1–36 for the ACT, 130–170 for the GRE, and 200–800 for the GMAT. Just like on the SHRM-CP and SHRM-SCP exams, the numbers of questions on these tests differ from their reported scores.

What Does a "200" Score Mean?

For the SHRM exams, 200 is not necessarily a perfect score. We do not report scores above 200 because anyone who passes the SHRM-CP or SHRM-SCP exam is considered to have achieved the competency level required to earn certification. We *could* just report a pass/fail result; instead, we provide all examinees with a score report that shows on a graph how well they did in each of three competency clusters and in each of three knowledge domains. This additional information can aid test takers in evaluating their strengths and weaknesses. Unsuccessful examinees have a numerical score to find out how close they were to being successful, plus a descriptive graphic to help them make appropriate choices about how to prepare for future exams. For successful examinees, the score report serves as feedback on their performance and can help guide their recertification plans and professional development activities.

The SHRM-CP and SHRM-SCP exams—like the PMP, SAT, ACT, GRE, and GMAT—have been developed using rigorous methodologies and procedures. The exams include a combination of low-, medium-, and high-difficulty questions. While we try to make sure the distribution of difficulty is the same on every exam, it is practically impossible to guarantee that each exam is precisely equal in terms of its difficulty. Therefore, we use a statistical process called equating to match the raw scores from a particular test with the scaled scores from that test. This is to ensure that examinees are not unfairly penalized or rewarded for having taken an exam form that was more or less difficult than another exam form given at another time for the same certification.

Equating is one reason why we cannot state the number of questions one needs to answer correctly to get a passing score. The number of correct questions you need to pass your exam form may differ slightly from the number of correct questions another examinee needs to pass an exam form administered during another testing window.

SHRM certification test takers are not compared against each other—that is, the exams are not scored on what is commonly known as a curve. (In technical terms, the exams are not "normed.") If everyone who takes their test meets the knowledge and competency standards, everyone will pass. The opposite is also true. If no one who takes the test meets the knowledge and competency standards, no one will pass.

If You Don't Pass

Do not feel discouraged if you do not pass the certification exam. It is a very challenging exam, and between 30 and 45 percent of exam takers do not pass on the first try.

Leverage the information on your score report. View the experience as a learning opportunity and use the information in your score report to refocus or reengineer a study plan that will help you prepare for retaking the SHRM-CP or SHRM-SCP exam. You can retake the exam as often as you wish by completing a new application, meeting all the eligibility requirements, and paying the exam fee.

Part 2

Study for Success

*"By admitting your inadequacies, you show that
you're self-aware enough to know your areas for
improvement—and secure enough to be open about them."*

–Adam Grant

To succeed on the SHRM-CP or SHRM-SCP exam, you have to know the subject matter that is being tested: the competencies and knowledge outlined in the SHRM BASK. There are two key ingredients. The first is your experience in the HR field. The second is a carefully designed and implemented study plan.

Start with your HR experience. Think about your job: what you do day in and day out, the different kinds of situations you deal with, the fires you put out, the problems you solve, and the initiatives you help to create. Consider the HR areas you are already familiar with because of your work: risk management, recruitment, workforce development, compensation plans, and more—all topics that are covered in the SHRM BASK.

Then create a study plan that will help you close the gaps between what you already know about HR and what you need to know to become a SHRM-certified HR professional. The better you have mastered the HR competencies and knowledge through experience and study, the better prepared you will be to pass the exam.

Start Early!

Wouldn't it be nice to have unlimited time to prepare for the certification exam? "Sure," you think, "but I'm already so busy. How am I going to find the time to study?"

Creating time to study in a busy schedule is one reason why it's important to get started well ahead of your exam date. According to SHRM statistics, most people who study on their own without taking a course spend 41–80 hours studying for the certification exam. Those who achieve the highest pass rate spend 81–120 hours studying. The average certification candidate spends a total of 70–80 hours preparing for the test, and most people start at least three to four months ahead of time. Approximately 10–15 percent of that time is spent identifying areas where they need to study most because they have not yet mastered the HR content.

But everyone is different. How much time you'll need depends partly on how much you already know through your education and experience and partly on how you prefer to learn. The strategies in this section can help you make the best use of your study time so you will be well prepared and full of confidence on test day.

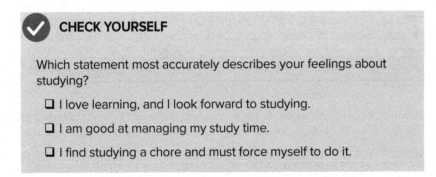

CHECK YOURSELF

Which statement most accurately describes your feelings about studying?

❑ I love learning, and I look forward to studying.

❑ I am good at managing my study time.

❑ I find studying a chore and must force myself to do it.

Chapter 4

Learning How You Learn Best

"Knowing yourself is the beginning of all wisdom."

–Aristotle

We're not all the same when it comes to learning (and in so many other ways as well). We receive and process information differently, and we like to learn in different ways.

Some people learn best by reading, taking notes by hand, and explaining the concepts to someone else. Others grasp new information and concepts more easily when the content is presented in visual form via charts, graphs, slides, and videos.

Understanding your learning preferences, or styles, will help you decide how best to study for success on the exam.

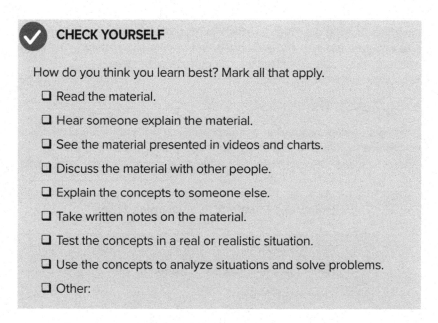

CHECK YOURSELF

How do you think you learn best? Mark all that apply.

❑ Read the material.

❑ Hear someone explain the material.

❑ See the material presented in videos and charts.

❑ Discuss the material with other people.

❑ Explain the concepts to someone else.

❑ Take written notes on the material.

❑ Test the concepts in a real or realistic situation.

❑ Use the concepts to analyze situations and solve problems.

❑ Other:

Four Primary Learning Styles

In 1982, management experts Peter Honey and Alan Mumford published a learning styles questionnaire based on psychologist David Kolb's learning style model. Honey and Mumford identified four primary types of learners: activists, reflectors, theorists, and pragmatists. No one is entirely one type or another, but most people prefer one or two of the four styles.

Activists (Doers)

If you're an activist, you have an open-minded approach to learning and enjoy experimenting, exploring, and discovering. Anxious to practice what you learn and apply it to real-world situations, you might become impatient with lengthy discussions and explanations. Some activists might have a tendency to be disorganized and to procrastinate.

Reflectors (Reviewers or Observers)

Reflectors prefer to learn by watching or listening. If you're a reflector, you like to take your time, collect data, and examine experiences or concepts from a number of different perspectives before coming to conclusions. You might have a tendency to dislike pressure and tight deadlines.

Theorists (Thinkers)

If facts, models, concepts, and systems help you engage in the learning process, you might be described as a theorist. You like to think things through, analyze what you are learning, and understand the underlying theory. You might also tend to be more organized than other types of learners.

Pragmatists (Planners)

You might describe yourself as a pragmatist if you enjoy solving problems and sometimes become impatient with too much theory and lengthy discussions. When you learn, you want to know how the concepts apply in the "real" world.

Honey and Mumford: Four Learning Styles

- Activists (Doers)
- Reflectors (Reviewers or Observers)
- Theorists (Thinkers)
- Pragmatists (Planners)

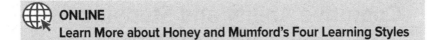

ONLINE
Learn More about Honey and Mumford's Four Learning Styles

https://www.open.edu/openlearn/ocw/pluginfile.php/629607/mod
_resource/content/1/t175_4_3.pdf

Three Ways to Learn

Researchers have also found that our learning styles differ in the ways in which we use our senses to receive and process information. One well-known theory, called "VAK," postulates that most of us learn best when using one or two of our three primary sensory receivers: visual, auditory, or kinesthetic.

Visual Learners

If you're a visual learner, you like to have information presented through pictures, charts, diagrams, lists of key learning points, infographics, videos, and other visual media. Taking notes and making visual maps helps you remember what you hear or read. Interestingly, some visual learners can visualize pages on which certain information appears.

Auditory Learners

You know that you are primarily an auditory learner if you remember more of what you learn when you hear something than when you see it. You might prefer lectures and podcasts to reading. Reading aloud to yourself or talking to others about what you learn can help fix facts and concepts in your mind.

Kinesthetic Learners

You can be described as a kinesthetic learner if you find it hard to sit still for long periods. You need to stand up and move around often to keep from losing your concentration. Keeping study periods short and focused, taking notes by hand, and building frequent breaks into your study schedule can help you learn.

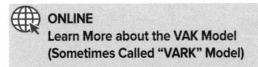

ONLINE
Learn More about the VAK Model
(Sometimes Called "VARK" Model)

https://vark-learn.com/introduction-to-vark
/the-vark-modalities/

Cognitive Ability and Studying for Different Levels of Questions

In Chapter 2, we discussed the differences between recall, understanding, problem-solving, and critical-evaluation knowledge items—the four levels in the depth of knowledge framework. A savvy test taker studies for a SHRM certification exam by preparing for questions at varying depths of knowledge using a variety of approaches.

Reading textbooks and studying vocabulary on flash cards can be helpful techniques—not only for answering recall questions that involve definitions, but also for higher level questions about the defined term. Test takers should be aware, however, that on a problem-solving question involving a certain term, for example, while knowing the definition of the term will help one understand what is being asked, knowing only the definition probably will not be enough to answer the question correctly.

Test takers can prepare for questions at higher cognitive levels by reading case studies, engaging in role-playing, and discussing best practices with a study group. These study techniques help one explore the benefits and consequences of actions, think about the most effective ways to solve real-life problems, and predict outcomes to guide organizations in making smart decisions.

SHRM Learning System

The SHRM Learning System offers a variety of formats and tools to help you prepare for the SHRM-CP or SHRM-SCP certification exam. Approximately two-thirds of certification candidates use the Learning System to prepare for an exam, and those candidates consistently pass at a higher rate than those who do not use the SHRM Learning System.

SHRM has designed several learning options to suit different learning styles, schedules, group sizes and locations. In addition to live and virtual classroom options, the Learning System is available in a fully online format. Real-life situations that require decision-making skills are incorporated into the online learning modules in addition to study tools to help you better understand, apply, and engage with behavioral competencies and HR knowledge.

Table 4.1 shows all the formats, so you can choose those that best fit your learning styles and preferences.

HR is a profession of *doing*. HR professionals create new strategies, negotiate salaries, communicate plans, and coach managers and employees. They roll out programs to increase employee engagement, boost inclusion, and reduce organizational risk.

When HR professionals prepare for their SHRM certification exams, however, they tend to use *visual* and *auditory* modes of learning. According to SHRM data, one of the most popular ways to study for SHRM certification is to read through the SHRM BASK. Other common approaches include reading the materials provided in the SHRM Learning System, reading while flipping through flash cards or taking practice tests, and listening during prep classes or study groups. While these methods are certainly helpful, they prioritize visual and auditory learning modes and miss out on the enormous benefits of kinesthetic learning.

Adding elements of kinesthetic learning to your certification study plan can be particularly useful for improving performance on situational judgment items.

The first step is to decide where to apply this learning style. In Part 2 of this book, you'll learn how to use the SHRM BASK to identify your strengths and areas for opportunity and put together a study plan. When you are creating your study plan, identify one or two areas that you want to explore further using kinesthetic learning.

The second step is to find specific ways to incorporate kinesthetic learning into your study plan for the areas you identified. Here are a few ideas to get you started:

- **Get on-the-job training.** Ask your manager about opportunities to learn by doing, such as shadowing a colleague on a project, joining a committee to address and solve an organizational problem, or cross-training on a process or system.

- **Seek out stretch projects.** Let your manager know you are interested in receiving a stretch assignment in one or more of the areas you identified. If possible, suggest a specific project that aligns with your goals and also supports the need of the organization.

- **Enact role-play scenarios.** Ask a colleague or mentor to act out realistic HR scenarios with you. Don't limit yourself to negative situations in which you resolve conflicts or address employee complaints—go for positive situations in which you demonstrate leadership and decision-making skills, too. For instance, you could present the business case for a new HRIS to an executive team or recommend actions to take based on the results of a training evaluation. Debrief with your colleague or mentor after each scenario, discussing what you did well, as well as other ways to approach such a situation in the future.

- **Gain off-the-job experience.** Use volunteer opportunities to gain experience in areas of HR that are outside of your expertise. Try offering ad-hoc HR support, or even just one-time advice, to a nonprofit organization, small business, or family member in need. Because you aren't being paid, you might feel less pressure and have more room for trial and error.

Table 4.1. SHRM Learning System Formats

Instructor-Led Preparation			
EDUCATION PARTNER PROGRAMS	CERTIFICATION PREP SEMINARS	SELF-STUDY PROGRAM	ORGANIZATIONAL TRAINING AND DEVELOPMENT
A traditional classroom setting, online format, or hybrid of the two—over a period of weeks or in a condensed format, led by a local, trusted training provider.	A virtual or in-person classroom environment with interactive and comprehensive discussions, activities, and preparation techniques from a SHRM-certified, expert instructor.	Study with our learning tools, where and how you want. Use SmartStudy tools to customize your learning.	Customized staff training at your location, virtually, or a hybrid of the two—eliminating costly travel expenses and time away from the office.
Ideal for *those who prefer a structured learning environment.*	**Ideal for** *those who prefer a structured learning environment.*	**Ideal for** *those who prefer to learn on their own schedule.*	**Ideal for** *organizations that are looking for a flexible education option.*

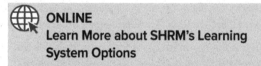

ONLINE
Learn More about SHRM's Learning System Options

https://www.shrm.org/certification/prepare/Pages/default.aspx

The SHRM Learning System Is Not the SHRM Exams—and Vice Versa

The SHRM BASK is the foundation for the SHRM-CP and SHRM-SCP exams. Thus, the exams test the SHRM BASK, not "books." The SHRM Learning System is not intended to be a replica of the exams, nor do the exams test how well you memorized the content or what percentage of practice questions were answered correctly in the SHRM Learning System.

Instead, the SHRM Learning System helps candidates prepare for the exams. It is designed to provide training content on all areas that are covered by the certification exams (i.e., the SHRM BASK). It also provides you with opportunities to answer practice questions that are similar to those found in the exams. Its study materials are intended to aid your understanding of the SHRM competencies, help you think in terms of real-life scenarios, and develop your situational judgment. Examinees are encouraged to focus not on the wording of each scenario but on the link between the competencies and their practical applications.

Updates to the SHRM BASK, which were based on the research findings of a validation survey, led to changes effective in 2022 for both the exams and the SHRM Learning System. Because SHRM is committed to maintaining the relevance of the SHRM-CP and SHRM-SCP credentials, it is committed to reviewing the content of the SHRM BASK every three to five years—the industry standard. We work continuously to improve both the certification exams and the SHRM Learning System.

SHRM Certification Professional Development Grant

HR professionals and students are encouraged to apply for SHRM Foundation Professional Development Grants. Recipients of the grant award receive one SHRM-CP or SHRM-SCP exam, as well as access to SHRM's online Learning System. For additional information, visit SHRMFoundation.org/scholarships or email SHRMScholarships@shrm.org.

Applications are accepted twice per year in advance of each testing window. See Table 4.2 for application deadlines and testing dates (and be sure to check the SHRM Foundation website for any changes to these dates).

Table 4.2. SHRM Foundation Certification Grant Application Deadlines

	First Testing Window Certification Grant	Second Testing Window Certification Grant
Application Opens	Second Tuesday in August	Second Tuesday in April
Application Closes	Second Wednesday in October	Second Wednesday in June
Testing Window	First testing window of the following calendar year	Second testing window of the following calendar year

Chapter 5

Use Proven Study Strategies

"Success is not final, failure is not fatal: it is the courage to continue that counts."

–Winston Churchill

For many of you, it's probably been a while since you've had to study for an important exam. To prepare for the certification exam, you need to get back into "study mode." The strategies in this chapter can make the difference between just studying and studying in a way that will pay off on exam day.

Keep a Positive Mindset

Imagine that two actors are preparing for the role of a lifetime. The actors are similar in terms of experience and skills. Which of them has the best chance of ending up with an award-winning performance?

✓ **CHECK YOURSELF**

Think back to some important exams you've taken. Which statements describe what you did to study?

❑ Took notes during class or a lecture.

❑ Read the material.

❑ Met with a study group.

❑ Watched a video.

❑ Attended a test prep class.

❑ Took a self-study course.

❑ Other:

Actor #1 worries that he isn't ready. Maybe, he thinks, he was cast in the role by mistake. Maybe he's just not good enough, and in time, everyone will notice and wish they had cast someone else.

Actor #2 firmly believes that this role is perfect for her. It will be a lot of work, she thinks, but she can't wait to get started, and she knows she will deliver a stunning performance.

There is a big difference between these two actors. It's their attitude.

Actor #1 approaches the role thinking, "I can't do this." With that attitude, chances are that he won't deliver more than a mediocre performance, if that.

Actor #2 has a very different mindset. Trusting her experience and skills, she thinks, "I *can* do this, and I can do it very well!" Her positive mindset sets her up for success as she begins the long and difficult process of learning the script and rehearsing for the role.

In terms of attitude, preparing for a certification exam is not unlike learning an acting role: if you don't believe you can pass, you set yourself up for failure. Negative thoughts like, "I can't do this" and "Other people are much better than I am" make it hard to study and to remember what you've learned on exam day.

But if you approach test preparation with trust in your experience and skills and the belief that you can do well, chances are that you will. You'll find it easier to put in the work to learn the material, cope with the frustrations that learning often involves, and step out of the wings on exam day prepared to deliver the performance of your life!

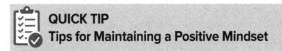

QUICK TIP
Tips for Maintaining a Positive Mindset

- Trust your experience and skills.
- Think "I can" instead of "I can't."
- Avoid comparing yourself to others.
- See the learning process as an opportunity, not a chore.
- Commit yourself to the study process and make it a top priority.

Learn Actively, Not Passively

Let's go back to the example of the actors. Actor #2 is approaching the preparation process with a positive mindset. But what if all she does to prepare is read the script and try to memorize the lines silently to herself? It's a good bet that she won't do a very good job. In fact, she's likely to forget many of the lines when she steps on the stage.

That's why actors prepare by reading their lines aloud, thinking about how their characters react to different situations, and rehearsing the scenes over and over again. In other words, the actors learn actively, not passively.

Learning experts know that passive learning, such as reading and rereading, highlighting, rote memorization, listening to lectures, and watching videos isn't enough for learners to be able to retain it. Like the actors, being able to retain the material and then to recall it when needed requires active learning. That means doing something with the material.

To learn actively,

» Read to remember.

» Look up unclear words and phrases.

» Develop outlines of the key facts and concepts.

» Use flash cards to help learn key terminology and facts.

» Discuss the material with other learners.

» Explain and teach the material to others.

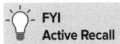

FYI
Active Recall

The process of learning in a way that helps you remember the information is sometimes called "active recall." It is based on the principle that in order to learn and remember the material, you need to stimulate your brain to recall it from your long-term memory when you need it—for example, when you're taking an exam.

Read to Remember

Reading is an essential part of studying. But unless you have a photographic memory, you probably forget all or most of what you read by the time you get back from a coffee break. To study effectively, you have to be able to remember what you read. There are a variety of ways to do that.

Skim What You're About to Read

Before you dive into reading a chapter or a section of the material, skim it. Don't try to understand or retain anything at this point—the purpose is to get an overview or a preview of the contents. Notice headings, text that is in boldface or italic type, and bulleted and numbered lists. Anything that is highlighted or stands out gives you clues to the content.

Take Smart Notes

Note-taking is a time-honored study tool. Taking notes helps you stay focused and engaged in the material, think critically about what you read, draw conclusions, and identify main ideas. But smart note-taking is more than dutifully copying from the text. The way you take notes should help you learn.

Here are some smart note-taking strategies to try:

» Read a short section—a couple of paragraphs, up to a page. Without looking back at the text, make notes from what you remember, trying to capture the main points in your own words. Then read the section again and fill in any important details you may have missed.

» Annotate the text. If you're reading something in print or using an electronic version that allows commenting, underline, circle, or highlight key words and phrases, and add your own comments.

» Look up unfamiliar words. It's very important to understand the terminology that you will find on the test. As you read, look up any words or acronyms you don't fully understand. Note the definition on the page and keep a separate list of terminology you need to study. Use the acronym list and glossary in the appendices of this book and in the SHRM BASK to review the meaning of key terms and concepts.

» Stop from time to time and think about what you're reading. Is the concept new to you, or are you already familiar with it from your own experience? In what ways might it be used or applied in the real world or on the exam? Remember that the SJIs on the exam are based on real workplace incidents encountered by HR professionals—the kinds of incidents you regularly have to handle at work. Consider how the situation presented in the scenario reflects a situation you've already experienced in your job.

» Write summaries. Writing a summary in your own words helps you focus on the most important information facts and concepts.

» Create a visual map. Also known as a mind map, a visual map is a flowchart or diagram of your notes. One way to do it is to place the main topic in the center of the page, with the subtopics and supporting details branching off (Figure 5.1).

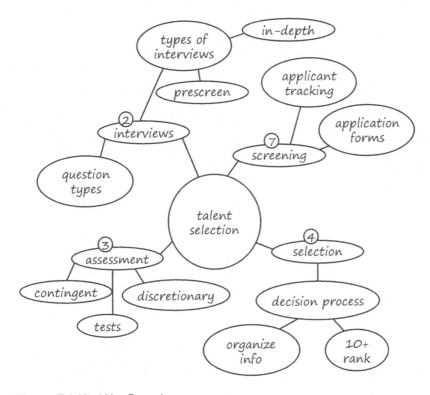

Figure 5.1. Mind Map Example

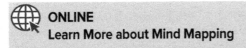 **ONLINE**
Learn More about Mind Mapping

"Mind Mapping," Student Services Information Desk, The University of Sheffield, https://www.sheffield.ac.uk/ssid/301/study-skills /everyday-skills/mind-mapping.

QUICK TIP
Your Experience: The Foundation

You don't start from zero when you begin to prepare for the SHRM certification exam. You either have been working in the HR field (perhaps for many years!) or you are interested in a career in HR, so you likely already know some of the facts and concepts that will be on the test. Keep your own experience in mind as you study by thinking about the content you're learning and how it relates to your own experience.

Use Flash Cards

If you've ever learned a new language, you know that flash cards can be a useful learning tool. Flash cards with key questions on the front and the answers on the back are terrific study tools that help you learn and see how well you are retaining what you learn. When you look at the first side of the card, you either know what's on the other side or you don't. If you don't, you'll know to keep working on that fact, term, acronym, or concept. However, please note that flash cards will likely not be the best way to learn behavioral competencies or to learn to effectively answer situational judgment items (Figure 5.2).

job enlargement	**process of broadening a job's scope by adding different tasks to the job.**

Figure 5.2. Flash Cards Example

The Leitner System

The Leitner System for using flash cards was developed by Austrian science writer Sebastian Leitner to improve his own ability to retain what he learned. Called "spaced repetition," it's a very powerful technique to help you recall what you study.

Leitner set up a box with several compartments. He put new flash cards in the first compartment and used them every day to test his recall of what he was learning. When he answered a question correctly, he moved the flash card to a second compartment.

Every two days, he tried again to answer the questions on the flash cards in the second compartment. The ones he got right moved to a third compartment, and the ones he got wrong moved back to the first compartment.

Several days later, he tried to answer the questions on the cards in the third compartment. This time, the ones he got wrong moved back to the first compartment and the ones he got right moved to a fourth compartment. As cards moved into "higher" compartments, he tested himself on those topics less and less frequently, focusing instead on the topics he had difficulty recalling.

Tips for Using Flash Cards

» Set up a box like Leitner's, with separate compartments, or create your own variation with single boxes or rubber bands that separate the levels of cards into packs.

» If you use the SHRM Learning System to help you prepare for the exam, you'll have access to a set of prepared flash cards. Otherwise, you can make your own. When you run across a term, fact, or concept that is new to you, write it on one side of a 3×5 or 4×6 card. Then write the answer or description on the other side. In fact, the process of creating your own flash cards can help you learn.

» Carry flash cards with you so you can test yourself while you're standing in line, waiting for an appointment, or have a few minutes of spare time. You'll be surprised by how much studying you do during those "dead" times.

 ONLINE

Put the words "create flash cards" into a web browser, and you'll find a variety of low-cost tools for making your own.

ONLINE
Learn More about Active Recall, the Leitner System, and the Feynman Technique

"What is Active Recall? How to Use It to Ace Your Exams," *Brainscape*, https://www.brainscape.com/academy/active-recall -definition-studying/

Robert Harris, "Learning Strategy 10: The Leitner Flash Card System," February 27, 2014, https://www.virtualsalt.com/learn10.html.

"Learning From the Feynman Technique," *Evernote* (blog), July 21, 2017, https://evernote.com/blog/learning-from-the-feynman -technique/.

Be the Teacher

A great way to see how well you understand and can recall what you're learning is to explain or teach it to others. Trying to convey facts and information to someone who knows little or nothing about the subject helps you quickly discover what you know well and what you need to work on.

The Feynman Technique

When he was a student at Princeton, Physicist Richard Feynman developed an active recall system that relied heavily on the idea of teaching what he was learning to a child.

> "A co-worker and I participated in a group training program through the local SHRM chapter. We both purchased the learning materials and combined [them] with the group sessions [which] provided additional support and interaction that more fully prepared us for the exam."

The idea is that teaching a child forces you to break down what you're learning and translate it into clear, simple language. You can do that only if you truly understand it. The process helps you remember what you've already learned and discover the gaps in your learning.

You don't have to have a child around to practice this technique. Your "student" can be anyone who is unfamiliar with the subject. Plan a lesson to teach something you're learning to that person. When you use your notes to "teach," you'll quickly discover how well you actually know the material.

Study with Others

✔ **CHECK YOURSELF**

Have you ever worked with a group to help you learn or to prepare for an exam? In what ways was the group helpful?

_____

_____

_____

_____

_____

_____

_____

_____

Studying with other learners can be a vital part of the learning process. In fact, researchers from other testing programs have found that people who study together in groups often succeed at a higher rate than students who study alone. Study group members help one another understand the material, review what they are learning, and identify gaps in their learning. They share resources and help one another build confidence as they prepare for the exam.

Study group members typically meet face-to-face, usually once or twice a week. But if there are not enough test takers for a face-to-face group in your area, you can find or form a virtual group with other HR professionals who are preparing for the same test. Your local SHRM chapter can help.

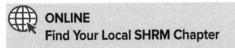

ONLINE
Find Your Local SHRM Chapter

https://www.shrm.org/search/pages
/LocalChapter.aspx

How Study Groups Can Help Prepare You for Answering SJIs

Study groups are particularly helpful to prepare for answering SJIs when group members work together to explore critical incidents in their own workplaces.

Here's how: Ask each member to present a critical incident that happened recently at work. For each incident, the group discusses . . .

» What happened, what HR issues (such as compensation or ethics) were involved, and what challenges the incident posed.

» What to consider when addressing the challenges, such as who was involved, time pressures, possible results of action or inaction, and so forth.

» What best practice would have been in the given situation. (Hint: Use the proficiency indicators in the SHRM BASK to help determine this!)

Tips for Making the Most of Study Group Time

» Choose group members who are studying for the same test, either the SHRM-CP or SHRM-SCP.

» Keep the group to a manageable size—three to five people is ideal.

» Have a specific agenda for each meeting that shows the topics to be covered, time allotted for each topic, who will bring what, and so on.

» Use assignments to encourage everyone to participate. For example, ask everyone to come prepared to explain or teach one topic to the others.

» Limit socializing to the first and last five minutes of the meeting.

» Schedule regular meetings, and try to schedule them for the same days and times.

» Choose a place that is free of distractions and where you are unlikely to be interrupted.

» For each meeting, choose a moderator who will step in as needed to keep the meeting on track and make sure everyone has a chance to participate. If needed, set time limits to keep one person from dominating discussions.

» Close each meeting by having everyone mention something they learned.

» Before the end of each meeting, set up the agenda and choose the moderator for the next one.

» Between meetings, use email or text to ask the other members questions that come up as you study.

» After each meeting, list the topics you do not fully know and understand and adjust your study plan as needed.

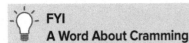

FYI
A Word About Cramming

Cramming is the practice of working furiously to try to absorb a lot of information in a short amount of time, usually just before a test. We've all done it when we have to take a test for which we haven't really studied. But researchers have found that learners are seldom able recall much information after cramming. Cramming just before a test can be a helpful way to review the material, but it takes dedicated study to learn.

Other Study Tips

» **Learn from former test takers**. People who have already earned their SHRM-CP or SHRM-SCP certification can be a great source of tips and advice. Because they have already gone through the process, they have the advantage of hindsight: what worked and what they wish they had done differently.

» **Take an exam preparation course.** The SHRM Learning System includes self-study and instructor-led courses, practice tests, flash cards, and more to help you prepare for the certification exam.

» **Pace yourself and take study breaks.** Studying takes an enormous amount of concentration and energy. Schedule breaks during your study sessions. Stand up and stretch, walk around, or get a snack. But avoid the temptation to distract yourself by checking your phone or email!

» **Make time for yourself.** Taking time away from study—from even thinking about the exam—not only helps you feel better, it keeps you from suffering "information overload." Make time for activities that you enjoy and that help you stay healthy. Relax with family and friends. Go for long walks or a run. Go to the gym, take a yoga class, or get a massage. Refreshing yourself helps you feel more relaxed, which in turn helps you concentrate on what you need to learn.

QUICK TIP
Study Best Practices

- Learn actively, not passively.
- Read to remember.
- Use flash cards to learn facts and terminology.
- Be the teacher.
- Study with others.
- Share experiences when preparing for SJIs.
- Learn from former test takers.
- Take an exam preparation course.
- Pace yourself and take study breaks.
- Make time for yourself.

ONLINE
Learn More about Using Flash Cards and Taking Notes

Thomas Frank, "How to Study Effectively with Flash Cards," July 26, 2016, YouTube video, 8:43, https://www.youtube.com/watch?v=mzCEJVtED0U.

Jennifer Gonzalez, "Note-taking: A Research Roundup," *Cult of Pedagogy* (blog), September 9, 2018, https://www.cultofpedagogy.com/note-taking/.

Crash Course, "Taking Notes: Crash Course Study Skills #1," August 8, 2017, YouTube video, 8:50, https://www.youtube.com/watch?v=E7CwqNHn_Ns.

Chapter 6

Where and When You Study Matters

"Your talents and abilities will improve over time, but for that you have to start."

–Martin Luther King

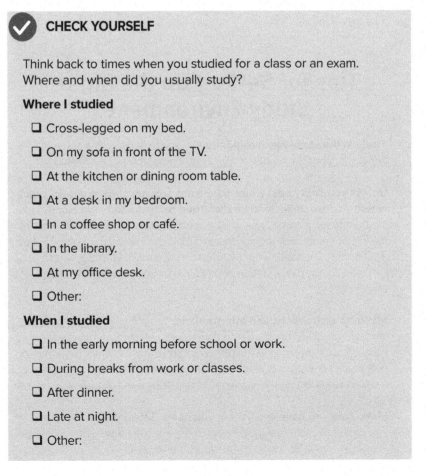

✓ CHECK YOURSELF

Think back to times when you studied for a class or an exam. Where and when did you usually study?

Where I studied

- ❏ Cross-legged on my bed.
- ❏ On my sofa in front of the TV.
- ❏ At the kitchen or dining room table.
- ❏ At a desk in my bedroom.
- ❏ In a coffee shop or café.
- ❏ In the library.
- ❏ At my office desk.
- ❏ Other:

When I studied

- ❏ In the early morning before school or work.
- ❏ During breaks from work or classes.
- ❏ After dinner.
- ❏ Late at night.
- ❏ Other:

Walk into any Starbucks, and you'll see people hard at work on laptops or with books and notepads next to their coffee cups. Some people concentrate well when other people are nearby, in front of the TV, late at night, or in brief periods between other activities. But most of us find it easier to focus on work or study in a place that is quiet, comfortable, and free of distractions; when we block out specific times for study; and when we are rested and alert.

QUICK TIP
Studying While Traveling

If your job involves a lot of travel, you might have to study while on the road, so you'll have to find a quiet place in which you can concentrate. Your hotel room will be private and, hopefully, quiet with few distractions. Most hotels also have quiet public spaces such as conference rooms or quiet lobby areas. If not, ask the hotel desk where to find a library.

Tips for Setting Up the Right Study Environment

» **Study in the same place regularly.** Once you decide on a place, it becomes "your" study place, the place where you expect to study.

» **Unless you study best when others are around, choose a quiet place where you are unlikely to be disturbed or distracted**—not a busy café, the company cafeteria, your desk during work hours, the sofa in front of the TV, or the kitchen table while your kids are awake. If you can't set up a study place at home, your local library probably has a spot where you can work, or maybe your company has a private room you can use in the off hours.

» **Minimize distractions and interruptions.** Turn off your phone (or leave it somewhere else). If you use the computer to study, turn off email notifications. If you're studying in the office or at home while family members or roommates are around, ask everyone not to disturb you. If necessary, put a sign on the door that says, "Working—please don't disturb me!"

» **Make sure you have everything you need.** Set up your study space so you don't have to interrupt yourself to get water to stay hydrated, snacks for extra energy, or coffee if you can't do without it.

» **Make yourself comfortable.** You'll need good light, a comfortable chair, enough room to spread out learning materials, pens or pencils, writing tablets, a laptop if you'll be using it, and so on. Arrange all those things ahead of time so you can focus on learning.

» **Keep a regular study schedule.** Set aside certain hours of each day for study just as you do for meals, sleep, and exercise. Choose a time of day when you'll feel rested and alert. If you work full-time, decide whether you're at your best early in the morning or in the evening. If you have free time during the day, decide whether you're at your best in the mornings or the afternoons. Also consider the times of day when you are least likely to be interrupted.

QUICK TIP
How to Decide Where and When to Study

- Study in the same place regularly.
- Study where you are unlikely to be disturbed or distracted.
- Minimize distractions and interruptions.
- Make sure you have everything you need.
- Make yourself comfortable.
- Keep a regular study schedule.

DIRECTIONS
Where and When Will You Study?

Where I will study:

_____

_____

_____

When I will study:

_____

_____

_____

Chapter 7

Create a Smart Study Plan

*"Good luck is when opportunity meets preparation, while
bad luck is when lack of preparation meets reality."*

–Eliyahu Goldratt

Imagine this: you have two weeks of vacation coming up. You've decided to
use that time to travel somewhere you've never been. You're very excited
about taking this trip, and you want it to be perfect!

But "perfect" doesn't just happen. Great trips require careful planning. You need
to decide where you will go, how you will get there, where you will stay, what
you will see and do, what to pack, and more. With careful planning, you can
leave on your trip relaxed and confident that you will have a wonderful time.

"Perfect" doesn't just happen when you prepare for an exam, either. It takes a
thoughtfully created study plan for you to be relaxed and confident on test day.
Your study plan will help you

» Make the best use of the time you have available to study,

» Set priorities so you focus on the right work at the right time, and

» Avoid procrastinating and keep yourself on track.

 QUICK TIP
Consider Your Available Time before Scheduling the Exam

To set yourself up for success, consider how much study time you'll
have available *before* you schedule the exam. It's better to wait for
the next exam window than to try cramming too much study into
too little time.

What Your Study Plan Should Include

A well-designed study plan includes the following:

» Your study **schedule**: a calendar showing the dates and times you have set aside for study, including time for study group meetings.

» Your **goal** for each study session. For example, you might want to be able to list the three most important . . . describe the best way to . . . explain what to do if . . .

» The **content** you will cover during each study session: the topics you will study to achieve your goal for that session.

» The **checkpoints** at which you will assess your progress: when you will take practice tests and make any necessary changes to your study plan to fill in your learning gaps.

A thorough study plan doesn't only include how you will learn the HR behaviors and knowledge you need for the exam; it also includes familiarizing yourself with the design of the exams. While you are studying, spend time learning and understanding the format of the exam. For instance, for SJIs, you will first see a screen with the scenario by itself, followed by one screen per question, which also includes the scenario. In this way, you can advance to the screen with all pertinent information on it (e.g., scenario, question, and response options) so that you can refer back to the scenario if needed. By knowing that the scenario will be repeated for each item, you will save yourself time from unnecessarily rereading it on each screen. Being aware of and comfortable with the functionality of the exam can help save you time on exam day and can also help reduce test anxiety. (For more on test anxiety, see Part 3.)

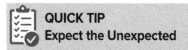

QUICK TIP
Expect the Unexpected

Things happen to throw the most carefully crafted study plan off track. You or a family member might get sick. There might be a crisis at work. It might take longer than you'd thought to learn a particular topic. Leave extra time in your study schedule so you can catch up if you get behind.

How to Create Your Study Plan

As we said earlier, the SHRM BASK is basis for the "blueprint" for both the SHRM-CP and SHRM-SCP exams. All the questions on the exam are based on the topics covered in the SHRM BASK. Thus, the purpose of studying is to close the gaps between what you already know from your experience in the HR field and what you need to know to become certified. That's why your study plan starts with identifying those gaps. Once you know what you need to learn, you can decide how to focus your study time and set up a workable study schedule.

Identify Your Strengths and Areas for Focus

Start by reading through the SHRM BASK to become familiar with the breadth and depth of content on the exam, as well as the format of the SHRM BASK.

Once you are familiar with the SHRM BASK in general, review one behavioral competency or functional area at a time. Read the definition, the subcompetencies (for behavioral competencies), the key concepts, and the proficiency indicators for the exam level you selected. Note the topics and terminology that you are already familiar with from your HR experience and those that are new to you or presented in a new way.

One effective way to do this is to review the SHRM BASK using highlighter pens (either on paper or electronically). For example, you could use one color to highlight topics in the SHRM BASK where your familiarity or knowledge is limited, then use a different color to highlight topics in the SHRM BASK where you have a solid command of knowledge for the topic area.

When you are reviewing the SHRM BASK, use the exam you selected to take (either the SHRM-CP or SHRM-SCP) to guide you. Most of the content in the SHRM BASK—including all of the behavioral competencies and functional areas—apply to HR professionals taking both exams. However, HR professionals at different levels need to demonstrate proficiency at different levels. Because of this, HR professionals who take the SHRM-CP are only responsible for proficiency indicators that are listed as "For All HR Professionals" under each behavioral competency and functional area. HR professionals who take the SHRM-SCP are responsible for the proficiency indicators listed as "For Advanced HR Professionals" and the "For All HR Professionals."

Next, think about your level of expertise in all the areas that are outlined. For the functional areas, this will primarily be the things that you "know," such as Learning & Development or Risk Management. To think through the behavioral competencies and how they manifest themselves in your daily work, think about situations, problems, and challenges you encounter at work. Think about how the different behavioral competencies are often used in tandem to approach and resolve issues. For example, Communication, Global Mindset, and Ethical Practice may all be needed to address an issue. Similarly, Business Acumen, Relationship Management, and Consultation may be combined to effectively resolve a problem.

Based on your level of expertise for each behavioral competency or functional area, rate yourself on a three-point scale:

» **Study most**: These are areas where you have little to no experience. If you primarily support employee relations and employee engagement, you may need to "study most" in areas such as talent acquisition or global mindset because you have little to no hands-on experience in this area.

» **Study some**: These are areas where you have some experience, but you're not an expert. This could apply if you are a generalist with experience across many (or even most) competencies; you might have a surface-level knowledge of the competency, but you need to spend some time studying to better understand that competency outside of just your role or organization. If you used to work in a specific area but now perform a different set of job duties, this might apply too.

» **Review**: These are the areas where you have the most experience. When you create your study plan, you don't want to spend too much time on these areas. Instead, you'll devote that time to studying the areas where you have more to learn.

When you are finished rating yourself, you should have twenty-three discrete ratings, one for each behavioral competency and functional area. Review your ratings and make notes about the terms, facts, and concepts that you need to learn or know more about so you can include them in your study plan.

It is important to review but not overstudy areas where your knowledge and familiarity with the content is already at a command-and-control level. Instead, focus your study efforts to improve your knowledge on the content with which you are least familiar. This means you should spend the majority of your study time on your "study most" areas, some time on your "study some" areas, and only a small amount of time on your "review" areas.

Once you have your completed self-assessment, group together the items on your checklist that you can study together to identify study "blocks." As you sort items into groups, list the related terms and acronyms. Once you've identified your study blocks, you'll have the outline for your study plan.

Set Up a Realistic Study Schedule

Your study schedule is a detailed calendar that shows when you will study specific items on your checklist (Figure 7.1). Here's how to create that schedule:

1. Figure out how many hours you will need to cover everything on your study checklist. Consider factors such as the extent of your HR experience and how quickly you tend to learn.

2. Determine how much of your time is already committed elsewhere. Consider the time you need for family, work, exercise, personal care, and social activities, along with "down time" and time for the unexpected, such as illness or a heavier-than-usual workload.

3. Decide how many hours of study time you will have available each week before the exam. If you plan to form or join a study group and/or take an exam prep course, identify how many hours each week you will need for those activities. Then divide the remaining time into study sessions.

4. Determine a specific, achievable goal for each study session and identify the content you will study so you can achieve that goal. Keep in mind that you'll need more study time for some content than for others and build time into your schedule for practice tests so that you can assess what you are learning.

5. Develop a realistic study schedule that shows your study sessions by date and time, the goal for each session, and the content you'll focus on during that session.

6. Create a week-by-week calendar that includes your scheduled activities for each day during your study period. Include time for

   > Family and friends,

   > Work (including your commute),

   > Scheduled appointments (doctors, dentists, etc.),

   > Exercise, and

   > Study sessions, study group meetings, and exam prep courses (if any).

7. Step back and review your calendar. How realistic is it? Did you leave time for meals and personal care, as well as some "down time" so you can rest and relax? Did you leave buffer time in case of the unexpected?

My study schedule for: [week] _____

Test date: _____

Goal: Become proficient in global and cultural effectiveness

Monday	Tuesday	Wednesday	Thursday	Friday	Saturday	Sunday
7:30–9:30 p.m.	7:30–9:30 p.m.	7:30–9:30 p.m.	7:30–9:30 p.m.	No study	10:00–noon	4:00–6:30 p.m.
Read Global Mindset Competency	*Focus*: strategies to develop global mindset; list skills needed for global HR	*Focus*: culture: definition, layers, theories	*Focus*: obstacles to cross-cultural understanding & strategies to negotiate cultural differences		Meet with study group 3:30–5:30 p.m. *Focus*: related terminology	Review and practice questions

Figure 7.1. Excerpt from Study Plan Calendar

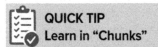

QUICK TIP
Learn in "Chunks"

Be careful not to try learning too much during any one session. Researchers have found that studying small "chunks" of content and repeatedly testing yourself on what you've learned helps you remember the information so you can recall it on exam day.

ONLINE

Kendra Cherry, "How the Chunking Technique Can Help Improve Your Memory," *Very Well Mind*, updated July 12, 2020, https://www.verywellmind.com/chunking-how-can-this-technique-improve-your-memory-2794969.

✓ CHECK YOURSELF

❑ I have a goal for each study session and have identified the content to cover so I can reach that goal.

❑ I have a realistic study schedule that considers my other responsibilities, myself, and the unexpected.

❑ I study at a time of day when I am most rested, alert, and able to concentrate.

❑ I have set up a regular, comfortable place to study where I am unlikely to be disturbed or distracted.

❑ I will take steps to minimize distractions and interruptions while I am studying.

❑ I will make studying a priority.

❑ Other:

Part 3

Sharpen Your Test-Taking Skills

"Believe in yourself! Have faith in your abilities! Without a humble but reasonable confidence in your own powers you cannot be successful or happy."

–Norman Vincent Peale

There are all kinds of urban legends about multiple-choice exams: the exam writers throw in questions to lead you in the wrong direction, the order in which responses appear provide clues about which option is the key, it's better to skip a question than make a wrong guess, a long answer is always more likely to be right than a short answer, the question isn't really asking what it seems to be asking—there's some hidden meaning, it pays to overthink the question because it can't be that straightforward, and more.

None of those statements are true about the SHRM-CP and SHRM-SCP exams (see Figure P3.1). There are no "trick" questions, and there is no "SHRM answer." You will not be given "none of the above" or "all of the above" choices. A response can be true but not necessarily right in the context of the question asked. There might be more than one effective response to questions posed about a situational judgment item based on a scenario, but only one will be best in the context presented. The order of the responses has nothing to do with whether a response is correct.

Myth	Myth Debunked
Myth #1 "Look for the SHRM answer."	**Incorrect**. Even though this "advice" appears in many social media discussions, it is absolutely *wrong*. Do **not** look for the "SHRM" answer. In short, there are no SHRM questions or SHRM answers because SHRM manages the process, but we do not write the questions. All the items on the SHRM exams are written by SHRM-certified HR professionals using the SHRM BASK™ as their guide, and the questions are rigorously validated to make sure that they accurately measure your HR knowledge. So instead of relying on this urban legend, use your reasoning skills, your HR experience, and what you've learned from studying to decide which responses to select.
Myth #2 "Look for clues to the right answer to a knowledge question—often the longest or shortest answer is correct."	**Also wrong**. Each SHRM-certified HR subject matter expert must write four plausible response options of approximately the same length. They are specifically told not to write "tricky" questions, so don't look for "clues" like the length of the response. There aren't any.
Myth #3 "I've got a lot of experience, so I can 'wing it'—I don't need to prepare."	**Not advisable**. SHRM research on the certification exams consistently shows that examinees who do not prepare for their exam pass at a much lower rate than anyone else. You need to know the subject matter, so leverage the resources you have and create a study plan to help you succeed.
Myth #4 "Situational judgment items scare me; I know I'm not going to do well on those."	**Shift your point of view**. Remember that you manage similar situations every day at work (or at least most of you do). Think about similar challenges you've encountered or problems you've solved—how did you decide which course of action to take in those situations? Think about best practices in HR. All these will help you prepare so you will feel more confident on test day.
Myth #5 "The exam automatically presents successively more difficult questions each time you answer a question correctly."	**Untrue**. Dynamic or adaptive exams present successively more difficult questions after an examinee answers the previous question correctly—but the SHRM exams are not dynamic exams. While there are standardized tests on the market that are dynamic exams (such as the GRE), the SHRM-CP and SHRM-SCP exams are not built this way and are not administered this way.

Figure P3.1. Dispelling Five Myths About the SHRM Certification Exam

Chapter 8

Practice Makes Perfect!

*"Practice does not make perfect. Only
perfect practice makes perfect."*

–Vince Lombardi

Roger Federer wasn't born a number one tennis player, and Yo-Yo Ma didn't just pick up a cello one day and start making beautiful music. It takes lots and lots of practice to master a skill.

Test taking is also a skill that takes practice to develop.

That's why it's important to take at least one practice test to become familiar with the different kinds of questions and the way they are asked. Practicing helps you answer the test questions more quickly and manage the testing time more effectively. Instead of trying to figure out what the test is all about, you can concentrate on recalling what you know so you can choose the right responses.

There is a forty-item practice test at the end of this book based on a combination of SHRM-CP and SHRM-SCP questions. If you decide to use the SHRM Learning System to help you prepare for the exam, you'll have more opportunities to practice. Note that the practice test in this book, as well as the official practice tests in the Learning System and other SHRM resources, are created with previously used exam items (also called "retired" items). These are the most realistic items that best represent the SHRM-CP and SHRM-SCP exams both from an HR content perspective, as well as in their style and format. Items that you find in other resources from outside of SHRM will likely be different from the types of items that are on the SHRM exams.

When and How to Take Practice Tests

It's important to choose the right time to start taking practice tests—not when you first start to study, before you've learned anything, but not too close to your testing date, so you'll have time to use the results to improve. If you can, take the practice tests on a computer, because that's the way you'll be tested in the exam room. You'll be able to answer some questions more quickly than others, but aim for an average of 1½ minutes per question.

There are three ways to take practice tests:

1. Untimed with access to your learning materials (open book).

2. Timed but still with open book.

3. Timed without any learning materials (closed book), as if you were in the test room.

QUICK TIP
Practice Timing the Test

When you take the SHRM exam, you'll have three hours and forty minutes to answer 134 questions. That breaks down to an average of about 1½ minutes per question. You'll be able to answer some questions much more quickly, leaving time for those you find more difficult. Timing yourself when you practice will help you develop a sense of how long it takes to answer both easy and difficult questions.

How to Get the Most Out of Practice Tests

» Figure out why you incorrectly answered a question, so you can pinpoint what you need to study. Did you get a fact or some terminology wrong? Did you not read a scenario carefully enough?

» What questions were you unsure of? Where did you have to guess? Feeling uncertain about which answer to select could indicate that you don't know that topic as well as you should.

» Take as many different official SHRM practice tests as you can.

» When you take timed, closed-book tests, resist the temptation to sneak glances at your learning materials. Put them away and take the test as if it were the real thing.

» Create your own practice tests. Write questions for topics that you don't fully know or understand. Put the "test" aside while you study those topics. Then try to answer the questions.

» Use the practice tests to practice using your HR knowledge *and* to practice your approach to answering questions. This is particularly true for SJIs because they are longer and more complex. See Chapter 9 for strategies on how to most effectively reason through an item.

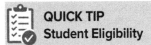

QUICK TIP
Student Eligibility

The SHRM Learning System has over one thousand practice questions that are similar to the SHRM exam questions.

ONLINE

Use online practice questions to get experience answering the types of questions you'll find on the certification exam: https://pages.shrm.org /certpracticequestions.

FYI

Sijia's Story: Valuing My Connection to the SHRM Certification Community

Professors and colleagues always cited SHRM as a trustworthy and resourceful HR community, so when I decided to become a certified practitioner, I chose to take the SHRM-CP exam. Now that I am a credential-holder, people from the US and other countries see those letters after my name and admire my achievement. For me, the true value of SHRM certification is finding myself in a larger community and the sense of belonging.

Preparing for the SHRM-CP exam took me back to my time in graduate school, when I was also reading, doing research, and sharing views with other students. The SHRM Body of Applied Skills and Knowledge (BASK) was a well-developed structure within which I could holistically strengthen my academic HR knowledge, as well as apply that knowledge to real-world client cases. Often during my exam prep, I found inspiring answers to client issues.

Support in My Career as a Consultant

I continue to find the SHRM competencies helpful in my work as a young professional in a big consulting firm in China. More company management teams are accepting the competency concept, which in turn (and more importantly) inspires HR practitioners to adopt the right skill sets for facing new challenges. Technical competencies are required by the job, but behavioral competencies enable HR professionals to become true business partners and create value for the organization.

The *Business Acumen* competency, for example, echoed recently throughout a client project involving HR transformation. My team facilitated a shift in mindset from responding to business requests to proactively thinking about business needs and providing services that deliver people-oriented value. That mindset shift was supported by my ability to understand the organization's strategy, operations, and external environments, the essence of business acumen.

With my SHRM-CP credential, I have gained the trust of clients looking for a consultant with global insights and a solid understanding of people and organizations. My proficiency in HR knowledge areas and the *Global Mindset* competency played a role in another recent project for a client that wanted to improve its employee experience across several geographic regions. I was able to help raise the client's awareness of the cultural and mindset differences between its regional leaders (who were mostly from the West) and local staff (who were located in countries across Asia that had quite different cultures and religions, despite being neighbors). The client was then able to place further emphasis on diversity in assessing the project's current status and in planning appropriate initiatives.

Recertification and Enriching HR Knowledge

Study never ends, even after one passes the certification exam.

I use my free time, usually while traveling to and from the office or clients' offices, to read SHRM's *HR Magazine* and newsletters and catch up with popular topics across industries. I also learn from the stories of other SHRM credential-holders to see how I might further elevate my career. At work, the SHRM website is the first resource I go to for insights and practice aids and what I recommend to colleagues and clients. The SHRM Connect online community is where HR peers discuss real issues we encounter daily, express diverse ideas, and debate possible solutions. I find the conversations inspiring, as they expose me to cases in the corporate world—a perfect supplement to my work in the consultancy world.

It was most exciting to be invited to join in SHRM-CP test-development activities and to work virtually with a diverse team. Since 2017 I have participated in several rounds of technical review, content validation, bias and cultural sensitivity review, and other important activities, which help to maintain a consistent and high standard for upcoming tests. Completing my assignments and submitting them on time are part of my commitment to HR professionalism.

When I lived in the Washington, DC, area, I saw the SHRM headquarters building in nearby Alexandria, VA, as a symbol of knowledge. Now, as a SHRM member living on the other side of the Pacific Ocean, each virtual meeting is a great opportunity for me to feel more connected to the larger community of SHRM-CP credential-holders.

—Sijia Bu, SHRM-CP

Chapter 9

Put On Your Thinking Cap: How to Reason through an Item

"The only place where your dream becomes possible is in your own thinking"

–Robert H. Schuller

The questions on SHRM's certification exams are designed to assess your expertise as an HR professional. Each question is written and thoroughly vetted by SHRM-certified HR experts in the field, and there are no "trick" questions on the exams. However, there are strategies that can help you decide which of the four possible answers to choose.

To determine which approaches to answer questions are most and least effective, SHRM conducted a series of item interviews with professionals during April and May 2021. These interviews included:

» Certified professionals who previously scored highly on the SHRM-CP or SHRM-SCP exam,

» Professionals who previously failed one of the SHRM exams, and

» Professionals who had never taken either SHRM certification exam.

During these interviews, a SHRM certification team member presented each professional with a series of previously used SHRM-CP and SHRM-SCP exam items. The SHRM team member carefully observed how these professionals approached each item, noted whether those strategies led to correct or incorrect answers, and looked for patterns in the results. The findings from these interviews heavily influenced the contents of this chapter in the book to make sure that you—a future SHRM certification examinee—are equipped with the best strategies for passing your exam.

Effective Test-Taking Strategies

Read Carefully Before Choosing an Answer

This seemingly simple advice will go a long way. The way you read the questions and response options before answering can make a significant difference. When you simply skim instead of reading thoroughly, you might misunderstand the question or miss something important in the question. This can lead you to choose a response that does not correctly answer the question.

For that reason, be sure to read the entire question and all the response options carefully. For example, if a question asks for a program, make sure your answer is a program. Similarly, if the question asks for a strategy or method, make sure that your answer is also a strategy or method.

For Knowledge Items (KIs)

*Read the Question First Then **All** the Response Options*
Read the question before you read the response options. While you are reading, look for key words or phrases in the question that suggest steps, process, or hierarchy. Pick out key words or phrases like "first," "immediately," "most important," or "most effective." Depending on the item, all the response options may be steps, important factors, and so forth. Your job is to select the one that correctly matches the key word or phrase in the question. If you are struggling with an item, flag it to return later. Remember to highlight key words or phrases about steps or hierarchy to help jog your memory when you return to it later.

Identify Key HR Terms
While you are reading, it is also important to identify key HR terms. Successful examinees identify key HR terms and consider what they know about that topic as they read. For example, if you're reading an item about succession planning, you might think to yourself, "This company is focused on succession planning, so I know they are thinking about building their talent pipeline." If you're reading an item about performing the last step in the ADDIE model, you might think to yourself, "I know the ADDIE model. Evaluation is the last step, and it is used to assess the quality and effectiveness of the training solution."

If you encounter a term that you don't know, use your detective skills to figure it out. Start by breaking it into parts to try to figure out what it might mean. This could mean looking at root words within the term or separate words in the phrase. During the item interviews, some participants weren't quite sure about the meaning of "product differentiation strategy." Those who broke the phrase down into parts were more likely to get the item correct. Here's an example of what this looks like:

"product differentiation strategy" =

"product" + "*different*iation" + "strategy" =

a "strategy" to make your "product" "different" or stand out in the market

For Situational Judgment Items (SJIs)

Read the Scenario First

Based on the results of the item interviews, SHRM recommends reading the entire scenario first. This is because reading the scenario gives you the context you need to fully understand an item. It can also be helpful to jot down key points using the virtual scratchpad on the Prometric testing platform or use the highlight feature as you read. A scenario may appear intimidating at first, but breaking it into digestible chunks helps you remember the relevant pieces as you read the response options.

Once you have read the scenario, then read the question and *all* of the response options. Do not stop at the first one you think might be right; there might be a better response among the other choices. Similarly, make sure to read every response option before eliminating any of them so that you fully understand the item. If you start eliminating options before you read all the options, you could eliminate them all and then have to start over.

There will be two or three questions about each scenario. Follow the same process of reading the question and all four response options before answering a question and moving on to the next item.

Narrow Down the Choices

After you read the entire question and all the answers, you might feel confident that only one of the answers is right. If so, select it and move on. If you're not sure, use the strikeout feature in the testing platform to eliminate any responses you are certain don't answer the question, are incorrect, or don't make sense. That way, you can focus on the answers that are more likely to be right. If you are still unsure of the answer after rereading the item, you should make your best guess and then flag the item and return to it later.

Reread the Item as Needed

When in doubt, go back to the question and reread it. If you struggle with an item or think there is more than one correct answer, pause and reread the scenario (if it's an SJI) and question. Look for key words, HR terms, or other details that you might have missed when you first read it.

Also keep in mind that it is normal to spend more time rereading toward the end of the exam. This might happen because (1) test fatigue starts to set in and you need to reread questions to make sure you understand them, or (2) you are reviewing items that you previously found challenging and flagged.

Once You've Decided on the Answer, Mentally Defend Your Choices

Know and understand why you chose your answer. Every knowledge item is developed by a SHRM-certified HR professional and must include a *rationale* that explains both why the correct answer is right and the other response options are wrong. This ensures there is only one correct answer to every knowledge item on the exams. When you are answering an item, use the same process. Justify to yourself why you selected your answer as correct and why you eliminated each of the other options. Use specific information or details from the stem or scenario to support your thinking.

During this process, you'll sometimes realize you don't have a concrete reason for your choice. This does not mean your decision is wrong, but it is a sign that you might want to review the question again! Either reread the item to help you refine your thoughts or flag the item to return to it at the end of the section.

Use Your Time Wisely

The SHRM-CP and SHRM-SCP exams are timed, but they are not speed tests. You do not get extra points for finishing early. There is no need to rush. The test is designed to provide ample time to answer all the questions, and the vast majority of examinees finish their exam in the allotted time. However, if you spend too much time on one question, your time could run out before you're able to finish your exam. Don't "watch the clock," but do periodically spot-check your time remaining.

This is where your experience and study come in. The more you know about the topics and the more practice questions you complete, the more confident you'll feel that you can answer all the questions within the allotted time.

If you finish the exam early, spend some extra time reviewing your answers. However, do not change an answer unless you are sure the first answer you selected is wrong.

There Is No Penalty for Guessing

No matter how well-prepared you are, some questions are bound to puzzle you. When this happens, don't panic or waste time going over the question and answer choices. Remember that you receive credit for selecting the correct answer, and you are not penalized if an answer is wrong. If you guess when you absolutely do not know the answer, you have a 25 percent chance of getting it right—and an even better chance if you've eliminated the obviously wrong answers first. If you don't answer the question, you have a zero percent chance of getting it right. So strike out the obviously wrong responses, make an educated guess, flag the question for review later, and read the next question.

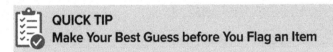

QUICK TIP
Make Your Best Guess before You Flag an Item

If you need to flag an item to return to later, make sure to choose an answer before you move on to the next question. In case you don't have time to return to it later, at least you haven't left it blank!

Once You Answer a Question, Move On

Don't waste time by second-guessing yourself. If you are not sure about an answer, mark the question for review and move on to the next. If you studied well and read both the question and the answer choices carefully, the odds are good that you will choose the right answer the first time. Resist the urge to change an answer unless you are confident you answered incorrectly when you first selected your answer.

Review Your Flagged Questions

Don't forget to revisit those challenging questions that you flagged. Once you answer all the questions, go back to those that you marked for review. Just as before, be careful not to spend too much time on a single question or second-guess yourself. If you decide to change your answer to a question, use the process of mentally defending your choice to be certain you answered it wrong initially. Read more about checking flagged items in Chapter 11.

Stay Calm

Don't be afraid to take a moment to pause if you need it. Even if you feel confident that you are ready for the test, you still might feel panicky or rushed, and that can lead you to make mistakes. If you feel yourself getting shaky or tense, sit back for a moment, close your eyes, and take several deep breaths to calm yourself.

Strategies to Avoid

Not only did the item interviews reveal strategies that can help you perform well on a SHRM certification exam, they also revealed strategies that should be avoided. In some situations, these strategies might slow you down a bit, while in others they could cause you to get answers wrong or even fail the exam.

We recommend avoiding these strategies while taking your exam, but also avoid using them when you are taking practice questions or practice tests. Don't "practice" bad habits!

Avoid Trying to Predict the Answer Based on the Question

Trying to predict the answer is not generally helpful because it wastes time. During the item interviews, many HR professionals who tried to predict the correct answer guessed answers that were not listed as one of the four options. As a result, they wasted time and spent more time trying to fit one of the response options into the answer they came up with in their head. This is particularly important for SJIs because there are many, many actions an HR professional could take and only four of them are listed as response options.

Predicting the answer based on the question can be a helpful strategy when facing a question at the recall level. For example, if you read the question and think, "X is the right method," you can look for that method among the answer choices. However, remember that only 15–20 percent of knowledge questions—or about 10 percent of all the questions—will be recall questions. Use this strategy judiciously, if at all.

Avoid Answering How You Would Respond to the Situation at Your Organization

The exam isn't designed to test information about *your* company, *your* industry, or *your* country. This means you should avoid selecting an answer simply because it aligns with how a problem was resolved in your organization. Instead, the SHRM certification exams are designed to assess how a competent HR professional who works anywhere in the world should act or information that any professional should know. Use the best practices that are outlined in the SHRM BASK to guide your thinking.

Avoid Assuming a Response Option Is Correct Because It Is True

It is easy to assume that a statement you know to be true is the correct answer. However, while an answer choice may be true in one context, it might not be the right answer to the question that's being asked. Be sure to read the question and then select the response that best answers that specific question. In other words, the response option needs to be both true *and* correctly answer the question. For an SJI, this means making sure that the answer you select is supported by the scenario. If a response option does not connect with the context of the scenario, then you should eliminate it.

Avoid Analyzing What the Question "Meant" To Ask

You can waste a lot of time overthinking questions, especially SJIs. Keep in mind all you have is the information given in the question. Take it at face value. While in real life, there might be different factors to consider with different ways to approach a situation, your job is to answer the specific question being asked. Do not overthink it or try to read into it; simply answer the question that is presented.

Avoid Getting Caught Up in the Details of the Scenario That Don't Pertain to a Question

You're not being tested on how much of the scenarios you can remember, so don't waste time trying to summarize every detail of a scenario while you read. In addition, there may be information in the scenario that helps you better understand the situation and the context in which it is occurring, or there may be information that is missing because it is not necessary. Do not get hung up on what you think is "missing information," because it would be provided if it were necessary to answer the question. Not every detail or phrase will be completely relevant to the questions you are asked, and not every nuance of the situation will be explained (or else the scenarios could go on for pages and pages!). Just like in real life, use the information you have available to you to make your best judgment. Don't allow contextual information to distract you from the question you are asked.

Avoid Looking for Clues between Test Questions, Especially SJI Questions That Share a Scenario

The test questions on the SHRM certification exams are designed to stand alone, and one question will not give you a hint about another question. In fact, there is a specific step in the exam review process to make sure this does not occur.

Examinees are most likely to erroneously look for clues when answering SJIs. For SJIs, each scenario will have two or three associated questions that depend on that same scenario. However, each question is independent and does not rely on the other questions in the set. Because of this, do not try to use your answer to one question to answer another question or check to see how your answers "flow" together. For example, if you recommend revising a policy or strategic initiative in one question, don't assume that revision occurred when you answer other questions in the same set. You should answer each SJI question based only on the information in the scenario and that specific question.

Avoid Changing Your Answer Because of a Pattern of Response Options

Do not get lulled into thinking there's a pattern to the correct answers. If you notice that you have selected a particular letter as the correct answer for several questions in a row (such as three, five, or even nine Cs), resist the urge to change your answers. SHRM uses a general range of how often each of the four response options (A, B, C, D) can be used as the key, but there is no exact "count." Trust your study and exam preparation, and always select the answer you feel is correct, regardless of whether it creates a pattern of response options.

Examples of Effectively Reasoning Through an Item

Phew, that's a lot! And all in three hours and forty minutes. So what does it look like to effectively and also efficiently reason through an item? Let's look at two questions from the SHRM's item interview research as examples.

Reasoning through a KI Example

Let's start with a knowledge item and learn how successful test takers considered and answered the question. (Remember, this is an exam item that is no longer used on SHRM-CP or SHRM-SCP exams, but it is representative of what examinees see on the exams today.)

> **1.** As a result of effectively promoting from within, organizations are most likely to spend comparatively more capital in which area?
>
>   A. Compensation
>
>   B. Talent acquisition
>
>   C. Learning and development
>
>   D. Onboarding

Successful test takers typically read through the question first. (Note that when we say "the question" here, we mean only the question and not the response options.) Then they read the question a second time to check whether they missed anything. While reading, they identified key words, phrases, or HR terms that helped them better understand the question. The following words or phrases stood out to effective test takers:

» *"Effectively promoting from within"*: Successful test takers often defined this phrase in their own words as "promoting employees internally" or "moving employees around in an organization." Some test takers also defined the phrase by thinking about its opposite, which is bringing new hires into an organization.

» *"More capital"*: Successful test takers often defined this phrase in their own words as "spending more money" or "investing more money."

» *"Most likely"* and *"comparatively"*: Test takers keyed in on these key words to help them understand that the question was not about absolutes—it is about what organizations are likely to do.

By combining these key words and phrases together, successful test takers recognized that among the four options ("comparatively"), the correct response is the area in which organizations are most likely to spend more money ("capital") when promoting internally ("from within").

Next, successful test takers read through all four response options. After reading through the response options once, successful test takers began to assess and eliminate responses. While assessing each response option, successful test takers are able to state a rationale or explanation for why each response option was correct or incorrect. Here are the common rationales that we heard from successful test takers during the item interviews:

» *A. Compensation*: At first glance, this response option is about money ("*capital*"), so it could be correct. However, it is traditionally more expensive to hire externally than it is to promote internally. A promoted employee who is brand new to a role will likely fall toward the lower end of a pay scale, while a new hire may have more experience and therefore earn higher compensation.

» *B. Talent acquisition*: Internal promotions do not require new talent acquisition efforts because the talent already exists in the organization. There are often lower costs associated with posting an open position for internal promotion, and the process of identifying talent requires fewer resources than recruiting a new employee externally. In fact, an organization is more likely to spend *less capital* on talent acquisition when promoting from within, so this response option doesn't make sense.

» *C. Learning and development*: Money that is spent on learning and development helps current employees grow and enhance the skills necessary to perform their role well and prepare for their next role. It makes sense to invest money into an employee to help them grow, and a newly promoted employee may require extra developmental support as the employee gains the knowledge, skills, and abilities to succeed at the higher level position. This answer makes sense.

» *D. Onboarding*: Onboarding occurs at the beginning of the employee life cycle. Because this question asks about internal promotions, the employee likely already went through the onboarding process. Based on this reasoning, this answer does not make sense because there would be no onboarding necessary when conducting an internal promotion.

By following this thinking, successful test takers correctly reasoned that C is the correct answer. The most important key words or phrases were "more capital" and "promoting from within," and C aligned with this well.

Reasoning Through an SJI Example

The process for reasoning through an SJI is similar, although a bit more time-consuming because there is more to read and understand. Let's see how successful test takers approach answering this type of question. (Remember, this is a real exam item that is no longer used on either the SHRM-CP or SHRM-SCP exam, but it is representative of items on current exams.)

Successful test takers read through the scenario first:

> An engagement survey at a global company reveals a widespread issue with the perceived fairness of the internal hiring process. According to the survey results, many employees feel the process is biased because candidates from the department with an open vacancy are typically selected over candidates from different departments, despite similar qualifications and competencies. This is because most departments in the company prefer to promote from within to keep employees engaged and ensure minimal investment in development for their roles.
>
> To support diversity and inclusion, the CEO requires all employees have the opportunity to apply for posted positions. For each posted position, hundreds of internal candidates apply. Many internal candidates do not meet the technical requirements of a role. Hiring managers are required to interview at least 10 candidates, and they complain this takes a significant amount of time away from their other duties.

After reading the scenario, successful test takers paused to think about and summarize what they read. They also considered their initial "gut reactions" to what they read. For example, during the item interviews many successful test takers remarked that interviewing at least ten candidates seemed excessive and time-consuming.

After they were sure they understood the information that was described in the scenario, they moved on to the question. (Remember that when we say "the question," we mean only the question and not the response options.):

> 2. Which action should HR take to immediately reduce bias in the process while maintaining the corporate culture of inclusiveness?
>
>   A. Lower the minimum technical requirements for job vacancies.
>
>   B. Create interview and inclusiveness training for hiring managers.
>
>   C. Draft a plan to implement cross-departmental panel interviews.
>
>   D. Limit the number of internal hires from within a department.

While reading, successful test takers identified key words, phrases, or HR terms that helped them better understand the question. The following words or phrases stood out to successful test takers:

> » *"Reduce bias"*: Using the information in both the scenario and the stem, successful test takers generally defined this phrase in their own words as "minimizing the preference that interviewers had toward employees from the same department."

> » *"Maintain a culture of inclusiveness"*: Using the information in both the scenario and the stem, successful test takers generally defined this phrase in their own words as "giving employees equal opportunity to apply for new roles, regardless of department."

> » *"While"*: Test takers keyed in on this word to help them understand that the question is about balance. The HR professional in the scenario needs to simultaneously reduce bias and maintain a culture of inclusiveness.

> » *"Immediately"*: Successful test takers clued in on this word as a term related to hierarchy and often defined this phrase in their own words as the action that an HR professional should take to "have an effect right away" or "have an effect most quickly." Many correctly predicted that several of the response options might be effective at reducing bias and maintaining inclusiveness but that the correct one would have the most immediate effect.

By combining these key words and phrases together, successful test takers recognized that among the four response options, the correct response is the action that balances reducing bias in the hiring process with maintaining the company's inclusive culture.

Next, successful test takers read through all four response options. After reading through the response options once, successful test takers began to eliminate response options while rereading them to further assess each option.

While assessing each response option, successful test takers could think of a rationale or explanation for why each response option was correct or incorrect. Here are the common rationales that we heard from successful test takers during the item interviews:

> » *A. Lower the minimum technical requirements for job vacancies.* The scenario and question are focused on bias in the process and not technical qualifications. Reducing technical qualifications is not a good idea because employees will not be able to perform required job duties. This is not an effective action.

» *B. Create interview and inclusiveness training for hiring managers.* This is an effective action that can help improve the interview process and increase inclusiveness. However, this action would not produce immediate results because it would take time to get stakeholder approval, create the training, and deliver it to hiring managers. Due to the timing, this is not the best answer.

» *C. Draft a plan to implement cross-departmental panel interviews.* Using cross-departmental panel interviews is an effective action to reduce bias and increase inclusiveness. Also, it would take less investment than creating interview and inclusiveness training. However, this action would not produce immediate results because it would take time to get draft a plan that describes the new process, get stakeholder approval, and implement the process. Due to the timing, this is not the best answer.

» *D. Limit the number of internal hires from within a department.* Because this action is similar to a quota, this can be implemented quickly and therefore produces the most immediate results. It reduces bias by not allowing hiring managers to only hire from within a department, which gives employees a more equal opportunity to apply and be selected.

Successful test takers correctly reasoned that D is the correct answer. This item is a great example of the importance of reading carefully. During the item interviews, many seasoned HR professionals picked B or C because these are generally effective workplace strategies. However, these do not address the need for an "immediate" solution and are therefore not the best answer.

Chapter 10

Anxiety and Procrastination

"Smile, breathe, and go slowly."

–Thich Nhat Hanh

Have you ever felt nervous or anxious before or during an important test? How did those feelings manifest themselves? Some describe anxiety as causing troubles with sleep cycles, shaking hands, upset stomach, accelerated heartbeat, difficulty breathing, lack of concentration, and panicking.

If you've ever felt nervous or anxious before or during a test, you are not alone. Taking a test is a form of performance, and performers of all kinds, from professional actors and musicians to conference presenters, often feel the symptoms of performance anxiety, or "stage fright."

Even though you don't have to stand up in front of people to take a professional test like the SHRM-CP or SHRM-SCP exam, you are being asked to demonstrate what you know. It is common for test takers to worry that they will not be able to perform well. The stakes are high; therefore, the anxiety is greater. For many people, a little anxiety can be a good thing. It can increase your focus and concentration and help you to do your best. However, for others, anxiety can lead to feelings of panic that result in what they most fear: failure.

The good news is that most test takers experience only mild symptoms that they can manage easily by understanding what causes their anxiety and learning how to reduce it. Even if you have a history of performance anxiety, you'll find that the strategies in this section can help you manage your symptoms, so you can focus your attention where it belongs: on the exam.

Understanding Test Anxiety

Test anxiety manifests itself in a variety of ways. The symptoms can vary considerably and range from mild to severe. Most of us have felt at least some of these symptoms at one time or another. You can't concentrate, and your mind races with negative thoughts. You have trouble sleeping. You feel nauseous; your mouth is dry, and your hands are sweaty and shaking; your heart races.

Those symptoms have a physical basis: they come from what psychologists call the "fight or flight response." When faced by a real or imaginary threat, the body releases adrenaline to prepare itself to either fight or run away from the threat. That was very useful when we were threatened by predators in the wild. It is not so helpful when preparing to take a certification exam.

Test anxiety can also create a type of "noise" in your brain that makes it difficult to recall information from your memory. That noise can make it hard to understand test questions and make reasoned judgments about which responses to select.

Why do some people experience little test anxiety, while others have so much anxiety they can hardly get through an exam? Here is some of what researchers found when they set out to discover the sources of test anxiety:

» **Parents' expectations and extent of parental support.** Research shows that you might feel more test anxiety when you're faced with a challenge as an adult if your parents had very high or unreasonable expectations for your achievement or gave you little emotional support when you faced difficult situations as a child.

» **Schools' increased reliance on testing.** Your early learning experiences can affect the way you feel about tests. For example, you might continue to feel anxious about tests well into adulthood if your teachers focused more on testing than on learning and pressured you to do well on tests for which you were not adequately prepared.

» **A fear of failure.** Whereas it is normal to feel some level of performance anxiety, you might experience much higher levels of test anxiety if you lack confidence or have very high standards for yourself and care a lot about what people think of you.

» **A history of performing poorly on tests.** It's a vicious cycle: you don't usually do well on tests, so you think you can't do well on tests, and, as a result, you actually don't do well on tests.

» **Being unprepared.** There's no doubt about it: taking a high-stakes exam when you haven't prepared is guaranteed to produce anxiety.

Strategies for Reducing Anxiety

"Before anything else, preparation is the key to success."

–Alexander Graham Bell

In this section, we discuss a variety of causes of and strategies to overcome test anxiety.

Test anxiety can come on unexpectedly, even for people with little history of nervousness about tests. This is especially true when the stakes are high and success is very important. However, there are steps you can take to keep anxiety from getting in the way of your performance on the SHRM certification exam.

Build Your Confidence by Preparing Thoroughly

You must prepare. Have you ever improvised at the last minute or run out of time to properly prepare for a major presentation? Think about how well or how badly that situation turned out for you. A certification exam is a serious undertaking, and preparing to take the exam is crucial.

The better you know and understand the material, the more you will feel confident you will be able to pass. That confidence makes it far less likely that high levels of anxiety could get in the way of your success.

Being more familiar with how the exam works can also increase your confidence. Reading about each type of question on the exam, completing the exam tutorial to see how the various features work (such as highlighting and strikethrough) and how items are displayed on the screen, and prereading the candidate agreement can help you be more confident about what to expect during the exam. You can also talk to other HR professionals who took an exam to learn about their experience and tips they recommend.

Don't wait until the last minute. Invest in yourself by setting aside the time to adequately prepare. Try not to overprepare, but do make sure you are comfortable with the subjects that might be tested on the exam, and make sure you allow yourself time to reflect on your work experiences.

There is no replacement for preparation. Embrace this simple truth and act accordingly!

Practice Realistic Thinking

The anxious mind is a very busy mind, and not in a good way. Test anxiety brings with it lots of negative thoughts that make it hard to think clearly. Instead, consider this: *thinking* something does not make it real. *Thinking* that you cannot possibly pass the exam does not mean you are destined to fail.

> "I wanted this certification so badly, so I really made it my second priority next to my day job. I took vacation days to study, which helped reduce my anxiety as the time approached. I also made sure I got enough sleep and exercise."

When those negative thoughts enter your mind, take a step back and examine them. Why is the test too difficult for you? Why won't you be able to pass? How do you know you cannot do well? After you examine negative thoughts more objectively, remind yourself that you have worked hard to prepare yourself for success. Every time a negative thought comes up, look at it realistically and tell yourself, "Yes, it's a challenging exam, but I am prepared to do my very best!"

Envision Success

Picture this: after you take the exam, you receive a letter that states "Congratulations. You passed." Envision succeeding and establish a roadmap to lead you to success. Plan well, and prepare for your exam experience. And when you get to the test center, take a deep breath. Leverage exam-preparation strategies to focus. This will help dispel anxieties.

Keep a Journal

One proven way to help manage anxiety is to write down your thoughts and feelings as test day approaches. Researchers have learned that writing about stressful events can improve ability to learn, solve problems, and more. Some have found this type of "expressive writing" has an effect on the capacity of your working memory.

Whether you choose to journal on paper or electronically, find a quiet place to record your thoughts and feelings in the weeks before test day. When you find yourself thinking negative thoughts, write them down, think about what is causing your negative thoughts, reason through them, and visual success instead.

Learn How to Calm Yourself

Even if you prepare thoroughly and feel confident that you know the material, you may suddenly feel nervous or anxious before or during the exam.

Learning how to calm yourself can help you concentrate. Try these techniques well before test day. Practice them early and access them when you need them.

» *Breathe slowly and deeply.* Experience shows that rapid and shallow breathing can make you feel tense. Learn to calm your breathing. Take several slow, deep breaths and let them out evenly and slowly. Focus attention on your breathing by "watching" the air move in and out of your body.

» *Tense, then relax your muscles.* Tightness in the shoulders and other muscle groups is a common response to stress. Practice relaxing your body. Shrug or roll your shoulders or gently roll your head from side to side and around in circles. If you do these kinds of exercises a few times daily, you will remember to use them if you start to feel tense in the exam room.

» *Visualize.* Find a quiet place and close your eyes. Visualize yourself walking into the test room, sitting down at the desk, and completing the test before returning your exam booklet and answer sheet to the proctor. Further visualize success by picturing yourself holding your SHRM-certified certificate in your hands.

» *Participate in activities that help you manage stress.* Studying for the exam is an intense process, and it can be helpful to do things that help you feel calmer or lower stress. You know yourself best; engage in activities that help you relax most.

Be Ready for Test Day

You are unlikely to feel relaxed if you spend all night before the test studying or if you have to rush to get to the testing center on time or cannot find a parking space when you get there. Be sure to get a good night's rest and eat a good meal before your scheduled exam time. Read through all the pre-exam communications that are sent to you so you know what to expect.

> "I followed advice from other test takers who passed, and I did not study the day before the exam. This is challenging to do, but it is very helpful to reduce stress and anxiety."

If you are taking the exam in person, make sure you know how to get to the test center, and plan to get there early so you do not feel rushed. When you arrive, engage with the proctor. If you feel nervous or tense as the test starts, use your breathing and relaxation techniques to calm yourself.

If you are taking the exam via remote proctor, make sure you know how to log into the testing platform and test your internet connection so you do not feel rushed.

📋 **QUICK TIP**
✅ **Managing Anxiety Checklist**

❏ Understand the reasons for test anxiety.

❏ Prepare thoroughly.

❏ Practice realistic thinking.

❏ Keep a journal.

❏ Learn how to calm yourself.

❏ Be ready for test day.

Procrastination

"The secret of getting ahead is getting started"

—Mark Twain

Do any of these statements describe the way you usually approach challenging projects?

❏   I spend a lot of time thinking about how to get started.

❏   I keep thinking that I'll get to it, and suddenly the deadline is staring me in the face.

❏   I work better at the last minute, so I put it off as long as possible.

These are common indicators of procrastination. Many people procrastinate periodically. For some people, however, procrastination is a lifelong problem. This behavior can take on various forms, but the general theme is leaving things until the very last minute, postponing studying, and struggling to meet deadlines. There is a cost associated with procrastination: decreased performance and increased anxiety. Objectively, procrastinating makes no sense:

your rational mind knows it is self-defeating. However, understanding the various reasons for procrastination that researchers have discovered and using proven ways to manage that tendency can help you change your behavior in order to accomplish your goals.

People Procrastinate When They Feel Overwhelmed

Imagine you have been asked to move your entire department of twenty-five people to a new building. Big, important projects like this can be overwhelming. "There is so much to do," you might think. "It's too much for me to tackle." Studying for an important exam like the SHRM-CP or the SHRM-SCP can feel the same way.

What to do

» To tackle any big project, break it down into a series of manageable tasks—it's much easier to do a series of tasks than to try doing everything at once. In fact, this is the purpose of a study plan.

» *Your* study plan is like the detailed plan a contractor follows to build the home shown in the architect's blueprints. It includes specific goals, action steps for achieving them, and a timetable for taking each action. Breaking down the process into manageable units makes the whole task less daunting.

People Procrastinate When They Have Trouble Managing Their Time

Everyone is very busy these days. There never seems to be enough time. Things always take longer than expected, and to-do lists keep growing. It can even be a major challenge to think about finding the time to study.

What to do

» One thing is certain: you cannot add more time to a day. What you can do is spend that time more wisely. Keeping a time log is a tool that may work for you. A time log helps you track how you spend your time so you can manage it more effectively.

» Whether you use a columnar tablet, a spreadsheet, or an app on your phone to set up your time log, as soon as you track all your activities for a week, you will see a pattern emerge of how you spend your time. Include time at work, commuting time, time with family, nonwork time, socializing . . . *everything*.

» Your time log will help you become aware of how you really use your time. You might notice that something you thought took a couple of hours actually took less than an hour to complete. Consider whether you are spending time doing things that do not need to be done or that could be done more efficiently. Thinking about these things will help you set priorities and reserve the time you need for study.

People Might Procrastinate Because They Are Afraid of Failure—Or Success

"I didn't study each night like I should have! Had I studied every night, I do not think the test would have been so stressful and I would not have had to cram in so much reading at the last minute. While I did pass the exam, I can be a testament to future classes that you really do need to study each night—and starting early is the way to go!"

A common reason for procrastinating is the fear of failing. Why try if you can't succeed? This thinking can apply to studying for an exam. Why study if you think you have no chance of passing? Surprisingly, *success* can also bring new challenges, higher performance expectations, more pressure, more stress. That can be scary. It can feel easier not to put in the effort in the first place.

A related reason for procrastination is the fear of not doing something perfectly. Achieving perfection is like trying to scale a wall that gets higher and higher as you climb. If you feel that there's no way to get over the top, why bother?

What to do

» Become aware of your fears and how they obstruct the path toward your goals. Remember that both failures and successes are opportunities to learn and grow.

» Instead of worrying about the bad things that could happen if you fail—or succeed—when taking the SHRM certification exam, focus on why certification is important to you. Think about the ways in which being certified will benefit you in your career as an HR professional. The more certain you are about the value of passing the test, the easier it will be to make studying for it a priority.

People Procrastinate Because It Has Become a Habit

Experienced procrastinators have honed the fine art of distracting themselves. Instead of working, they check their phones and email, think about what to have for dinner, find someone to chat with, rearrange their workspace, browse the internet, clean out the refrigerator, and do myriad other time-wasting things. Then they look up at the clock and wonder where all the time has gone.

What to do

» Stopping any bad habit takes a determined effort.

» Try this: Write down all the ways in which you distract yourself while you are working or studying. Post the list prominently in your workspace or study space and add to it if you find a new distraction.

» When you begin a study session, remove the obvious distractors such as your phone and internet access. Make yourself comfortable with water, coffee, or a snack close at hand if needed. Whenever you think about or do something other than studying, stop for a moment, take a deep breath, remind yourself of how important it is to achieve your goals, and then turn your attention back to your study plan.

» Breaking a bad habit can also be easier when you reward yourself for your accomplishments. Give yourself a reward when you reach milestones on your study plan. Put some money each week into a "rewards" jar to spend after you reach your final goal: taking the certification exam!

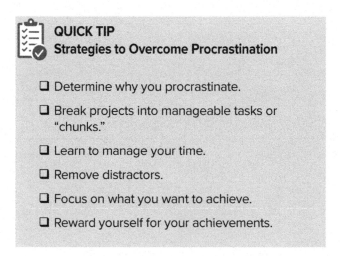

QUICK TIP
Strategies to Overcome Procrastination

❑ Determine why you procrastinate.

❑ Break projects into manageable tasks or "chunks."

❑ Learn to manage your time.

❑ Remove distractors.

❑ Focus on what you want to achieve.

❑ Reward yourself for your achievements.

Part 4

Exam Day

Chapter 11

What to Expect on Exam Day

*"Success depends upon previous preparation, and
without such preparation there is sure to be failure."*

–Confucius

You've worked diligently to prepare for the certification exam, and now the big day is almost here. Knowing what to expect can help you feel more comfortable and less nervous. Your experience on exam day depends somewhat on how you choose to take your exam. If you choose to take the exam in person, your SHRM certification exam will be held at one of Prometric's highly secure testing centers. If you choose to take the exam via remote proctoring, you will take the exam from the comfort of your own home or office using Prometric's ProProctor system.

Regardless of which testing method and certification exam you choose, the format of your exam and the level of test security will be the same on test day.

In-Person Testing

Prometric operates hundreds of test centers in more than fifty countries, typically in secure testing centers located in office buildings and on college campuses. If you choose to take your exam in-person at a Prometric test center, follow these tips to help ensure a smooth experience.

Get to the Test Center Early

It's essential to arrive at the test center on time. The test center administrator (TCA) can deny access to individuals who arrive late for an exam. If that happens, you'll need to reapply for the exam and pay another fee.

Arrive at the test center at least thirty minutes early so you can settle in and be ready to go when your exam starts. It's a good idea to do a "dry run" a few days before your exam: drive or take public transportation to the test center and note how long it takes you. If you'll be driving, figure out where to park. Then leave extra time in case traffic is heavy or public transit is slow on test day.

Checking in at the Test Center

When you arrive at the test center, the TCA will check you in. The TCA will ask you to show a valid photo identification (ID) and sign a logbook. Be sure you reread your Authorization-to-Test (ATT) letter and review the Prometric website about acceptable forms of ID. Your photo ID must be current, so check it far in advance of your test date in case it is getting ready to expire.

You can expect a high level of security inside the testing center (not unlike the security you encounter at an airport). Bring only what you need into the testing center because you'll need to leave all your personal belongings except your ID, eyeglasses, and locker key in a locker. This includes your phone and any jewelry except wedding and engagement rings.

Before you enter the testing room, the TCA will inspect your eyeglasses, hair clips, ties, face coverings, and any other accessories to look for camera devices that could be used to capture exam content. It's a good idea to leave such items as ornate clips, combs, barrettes, headbands, tie clips, and cuff links behind because you might not be allowed to wear them into the testing room. The TCA might ask you to turn out your pockets, and you might also be "wanded" or asked to go through a metal detector.

Although these inspections are thorough, they take only a few minutes. They will be repeated when you return from a break to ensure you do not violate any security protocols.

QUICK TIP
Ask for a Noise-Canceling Headset

Blocking out noise can help you concentrate during the exam. If you would like to minimize the sounds around you during your exam, you can ask for a noise-canceling headset when you check in.

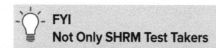

FYI
Not Only SHRM Test Takers

Not everyone at the testing center will be taking a SHRM certification exam. In fact, the person on one side of you might be taking an accounting exam while the person on your other side might be taking a cosmetology exam. The various exams are likely to take differing amounts of time, so you can expect that people taking other exams will come and go during your exam period.

Your Exam Computer and Station

Once you are checked in, the TCA will guide you to a seat at an exam computer. Make yourself comfortable and familiarize yourself with the feel of the keyboard and mouse. Use the time before the exam starts to take the exam tutorial so you'll be familiar with the computer navigation functions, especially the features for striking out obviously incorrect responses and marking or flagging questions you want to return to for review.

Live Remote Proctoring

If you select to take your exam via live remote proctoring, you will receive an appointment confirmation email with important information and links. Take time at least one day before your scheduled exam date to read through the information, (re)complete the system compatibility check, and download the ProProctor application.

You should expect a high level of security during your exam, just like if you were taking the exam in-person at a Prometric test center.

Prepare Your Testing Room In Advance

During a remote-proctored exam, the room where you take your exam *becomes* a test center. Because of this, your testing environment is subject to strict rules to ensure the security of the exam content.

When you are selecting and preparing your testing environment, keep in mind:

» Your testing locations must be indoors (walled), be well lit, have a closed door, and be free from background noise and disruptions.

» The entrance to the room must be in full view of the camera.

» Your workstation and surrounding area, including the walls, must be free of materials such as pictures, office supplies, or electronic devices.

Start preparing your testing environment at least a few hours ahead of time by tidying up and removing prohibited items from the room. This includes cleaning off your desk and removing extra technology, like a docking station or extra monitors. If you are unable to remove a larger item from the room, such as a bookcase full of books, use a sheet or other linen to cover it.

(Re)take the System Readiness Check

You should have taken the system readiness check before deciding to use remote proctoring. Take a few minutes before your exam date to rerun it (or if you didn't run it before, to run it for the first time). This readiness check lets you know whether your operating system is compatible to install and run ProProctor, which is the application that is used to deliver remote proctored exams from Prometric.

Once your compatibility check is complete, enter your confirmation number and surname to download the ProProctor application. If you downloaded the application previously, enter your confirmation details to ensure you have the most up-to-date software.

Log In to Your Exam

Just before you log in, perform one final check on your testing environment. Remove all unnecessary items or personal belongings from the room, such as books and extra technology. This includes your cell phone! You are not allowed to have your cell phone in the room during your exam. Consider placing your cell phone just outside of the closed door so that you can quickly access it if you run into technology issues during your exam.

Make sure to remove any jewelry you are wearing as well, except wedding and engagement rings. Keep only what you need in the room with you where you plan to complete your exam, including your computer, ID, and eyeglasses.

Once you log into the ProProctor system, you will first complete an identification check. This will include taking a digital picture of your valid photo ID. Be sure you reread your ATT letter and review the Prometric website about acceptable forms of ID. Your photo ID must be current, so check it far in advance of your test date in case it is getting ready to expire.

Next, you will complete the security check-in process. A Prometric readiness agent will confirm your name, address, and exam details with you via video chat. The readiness agent will ask you to provide a 360° view of your environment using your webcam. Your agent also will ask you to scan your work surface using your webcam. During this step, your readiness agent will ask to inspect things such as bookshelves, wall hangings, and electronic devices such as televisions. Your readiness agent will ask you to stand up to do a scan of your body. This scan will include—but is not limited to—conducting a sleeve, pocket, and glasses check. Additionally, you will be asked to turn all pockets inside out. If the agent identifies unapproved items, you must either remove them from the room or cover them up. It is useful to have a large bedsheet or linen handy in case you are asked to cover an area of clutter or unapproved items.

Although these inspections are thorough, they take only a few minutes. If you take a break during the exam, they will be repeated when you return from your break to ensure you still comply with the security protocols.

Once your security check is complete, you will be passed to your proctor. Your testing session will be monitored by a qualified proctor through audio-video and screen-share feed in real time. If you need assistance during your exam or wish to take an unscheduled break, type a chat to your proctor.

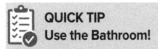

QUICK TIP
Use the Bathroom!

It's a good idea to use the bathroom before you begin your exam. The certification exam is four hours long, and there are no scheduled breaks. You may take one unscheduled break if you need it, but you will have to go through security again and will not be given extra time on the exam. That said, if you have extra time at the end of the first half of your exam, it might be a good idea to take an unscheduled break to use the restroom, splash water on your face, stretch, or loosen up tense shoulders.

Acceptable Forms of Identification

Be sure you read your ATT letter and review the Prometric website to learn about acceptable forms of ID. Your photo ID must be current, so check it far in advance of your test date in case it is getting ready to expire (Table 11.1).

Table 11.1. Acceptable Forms of Identification

Primary ID	Secondary ID
Driver's license	Valid employer identification card
Passport	Valid credit card with signature
Military ID	Valid bank card with photo

Examples of Acceptable Names on Required ID

Name on Application	Name on ID	Admitted to Test?
Jamie Taylor-Smith	Jamie Smith	Yes
Nancy Porter	Nancy White	No
William B. Johnson	Bill Johnson	No
P. J. Miller	Peter J. Miller	Yes
Samantha R. Roberts	Samantha Rose Roberts	Yes

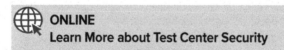

ONLINE
Learn More about Test Center Security

https://www.prometric.com/test-center-security

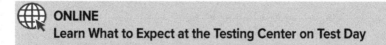

ONLINE
Learn What to Expect at the Testing Center on Test Day

https://www.prometric.com/prepare-for-test-day

https://www.prometric.com/test-takers/what-expect

Testing Accommodations

SHRM is fully committed to ensuring access to the SHRM-CP and SHRM-SCP certification exams for all individuals with disabilities covered by the Americans with Disabilities Act (or the Canadian/Australian equivalent).

SHRM provides reasonable accommodations to individuals with documented disabilities who demonstrate a need for special accommodations. Requests for special accommodations are inherently individualized and considered on a case-by-case basis. Therefore, no single type of accommodation will be appropriate for all individuals with disabilities. Common accommodation requests include extended time (either time-and-a-half or double-time) or testing in a separate room to reduce distractions.

All accommodation requests must be made at the time of application for an exam. To request an accommodation, the individual seeking an accommodation must complete a form and have a qualified licensed professional complete the professional evaluation. The professional must be an individual qualified to assess, diagnose, and treat the stated disability. Any information and documentation provided regarding the disability and the need for accommodation in testing will be kept strictly confidential and will be shared only to the extent necessary with our testing vendor.

For more information about testing accommodations, see the SHRM Certification Handbook at https://pages.shrm.org/certhandbook.

Rescheduling Your Exam

If you can't make your original test date, you can reschedule the exam. There's no charge if you reschedule within the same testing window at least thirty days before the test date. Prometric charges a fee if you need to reschedule less than thirty days before the test date. If you cancel less than five days before the test or fail to show up at your scheduled time, you will forfeit the fees and need to reapply for another exam window (Table 11.2).

In cases of extreme weather or a national emergency, Prometric may need to cancel the exam. In that case, Prometric will reschedule you as possible, and you won't be charged a fee for rescheduling.

Table 11.2. Rescheduling Exam Appointments

Time Frame	Reschedule Permitted	Stipulations
Requests submitted thirty days or more before original appointment	Yes	None
Requests submitted five to twenty-nine days before original appointment	Yes	Candidate must pay Prometric a cancellation fee of $53.00.
Requests submitted less than five days before original appointment	No	Candidate is considered a "no-show," will forfeits all fees, and will have to reapply and pay the fees for a future exam window.

Top Tips for Test Day

Before Your Exam

» **Get a good night's sleep the night before your exam.** Do not cram the night before your exam.

» **Eat a light, healthy meal.** Aim for a well-rounded meal that includes protein, carbohydrates, and fats to keep your energy steady during the exam.

» **Use the restroom.**

» **Plan out your break.** (Remember, the clock keeps ticking even while you are on your break!)

> > If you are taking your exam at a Prometric test center, ask where the restroom is located when you arrive. If you take a break to use the restroom during your exam, knowing how to access the restroom minimizes the amount of time you are away from your test.

> > If you are taking your exam via remote proctor, place water and food outside your exam room so you can grab it quickly.

During Your Exam

» **Use your test-taking tips and relaxation strategies.** Take deep calming breaths as needed. Stay focused and think positively. And keep the other strategies mentioned in Part 3 in mind as you complete your exam.

» **Keep your eye on the time.** Once you begin your exam, there will be a timer on every screen to remind you about how much time you have left for that section. Do not rush through the exam, but look at the timer periodically to make sure you are still on track. If you're not, you should speed up your pace as needed.

» **Use the relevant features in the exam interface.** Use the virtual scratch-pad feature to make notes or write down key information as needed. Use the highlight and strikethrough features as you read the test questions to help you select the right answer. Use the on-screen calculator for any calculations.

» **Be thoughtful about when you choose to take your break.** Let's say that you just finished the first half of your exam and checked all your flagged items. You kept up a good pace as you answered questions, and you have about twenty minutes of your one hour and fifty minutes left for the section. On to the second half, right? Not so fast! If you plan to take a break during the exam and you have extra time left at the end of your first section, take your break *now* before moving into the second half. This is because your exam time clock continues to run while you are on a break, and remaining time does not roll over to the next section. In this scenario, you could take a fifteen-minute break and still have five minutes of exam time left (minus time spent going through the security check) before moving into the second half. If you start the second half and then take your break, the time you spend on your break will count toward the one hour and fifty minutes you are allotted for the second half.

» **Spend your break time wisely.** Splash water on your face if it feels good or helps refresh you. Spend a few minutes moving your body if you want, such as taking a short walk outdoors. If you are taking the exam remotely, this could also mean doing a few yoga stretches or even playing with a pet. Give your brain a few minutes to decompress.

After Your Exam

No matter the results, reward yourself for finishing the exam! Taking a SHRM certification exam is hard work. Regardless of your result, take time to celebrate your effort with a delicious meal, time off from work, a new (non-HR related!) book, or another meaningful activity or reward. You deserve it!

Chapter 12

During and After Your Exam

"Anyone who stops learning is old, whether at 20 years old or 80."

–Henry Ford

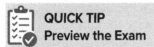

QUICK TIP
Preview the Exam

You can preview the exam tutorial ahead of time from your home or office computer. The tutorial explains the various features and lets you practice answering questions as well as using the features for striking out responses and flagging questions for review. You can access the tutorial at

https://www.prometric.com/sites/default/files /SHRM-Tutorial/launch_assessment_delivery.html

During Your Exam

As you take the exam, use the strategies and tips in Chapter 10 to manage your time and stay relaxed. If you need help or need to take a break, let Prometric know. If you are in a Prometric testing center, raise your hand and the TCA will come over. If you are taking the exam via remote proctor, send a message to your proctor using the chat feature.

Timing the Exam

The total exam time is four hours, including opening and closing activities. You will have three hours and forty minutes to answer the 134 multiple-choice questions on the exam itself. The exam is divided into two halves, so you will have one hour and fifty minutes to answer the first 67 multiple-choice questions and another one hour and fifty minutes to answer the second 67 multiple-choice questions. Make sure you review all flagged or unanswered items before you finish each half. Once you finish the first half, you won't be able to go back to it later.

The countdown timer on the screen will help you keep track of the time as you progress through the two sections. You cannot carry over unused time from one section and save it to use in another section. For example, if you have fifteen minutes left at the end of the first half, you will still only have one hour and fifty minutes to answer the questions in the second half. You cannot carry those unused fifteen minutes over to the second half.

Although it's important to stay aware of the time, you don't need to feel rushed. SHRM research shows that the vast majority of examinees have enough time to complete the exam without rushing, and almost everyone completes all of the items. You will have enough time to answer all the questions and take another look at those you've marked for review.

Pay Attention to Pop-up Messages on the Screen and Don't Click on "Finish" until You're Done!

Pop-up warnings often occur when you've hit a stray key and the computer thinks you want to finish the exam. The system asks you at least twice to confirm that you understand that if you keep clicking "Yes," you want to finish. Also, the "Finish" button in the navigation bar does not finish your review of the questions you've flagged for another look—it ends the entire exam. After you click "Finish," a pop-up window will appear asking you to confirm that you are done.

DO NOT end the exam until you are sure that you are finished. You cannot return to it once you exit. When a pop-up appears, pause, read it thoroughly, and then click the button that indicates what you want to do. DO NOT rush through the prompts, because each asks you to confirm your real intent but in a slightly different way.

If, after multiple warnings, you exit the exam, but did not mean to do so, there is no turning back. Once you confirm, you are at the point of no return and the exam will be over.

When You Finish Your Exam

Once your exam time is up or you hit "Finish" and confirmed that you are done, a short post-exam survey will appear on your screen. The brief survey helps SHRM learn more about test takers' opinions about the exam, reasons for pursuing certification, study and preparation methods, and current jobs. Your responses to survey questions do not affect your test results.

After you finish the survey, the system will give you an immediate "Pass" or "Did Not Pass" notification. Prometric will also send you a copy of the results by email, which you can share with others (including on social media). Be sure to check your spam folder if the email doesn't arrive.

Regardless of the results, congratulate yourself! Completing this rigorous test is a significant accomplishment, and you deserve a reward for all your hard work, so do something nice for yourself!

After Your Exam: Next Steps

Your Official Score Report

About two to three weeks after your exam, you will receive an email from SHRM about your official SHRM-CP or SHRM-SCP score report. An electronic copy of your official score report will be posted in your SHRM portal account. This report includes your scaled score (from 120 to 200), as well as feedback on how well you scored on the three knowledge domains (People, Organization, and Workplace) and three competency clusters (Interpersonal, Leadership, and Business). You can use this information to plan professional activities that support your learning and earn credits toward your recertification.

If you did not pass the exam, you can use this information to refocus your study plan to retake the SHRM-CP or SHRM-SCP exam in a future testing window.

You Passed! Your SHRM-Certified Certificate and Digital Badge

A soft copy of your new SHRM certification certificate will also be posted in your SHRM portal account with your official results report. You will also receive an email from Credly issuing your digital badge. You must accept the digital badge in order to share it on social media, such as on LinkedIn.

You Passed! Maintain Your Certification through Recertification

Achieving certification sets you on the path to continuous learning and career development. Maintaining your certification helps you keep your knowledge, skills, and abilities relevant.

To maintain your certification, you will need to earn sixty professional development credits (PDCs) within each three-year period. Credits are awarded for your study, your experience, and your contributions in three categories: Education, Profession, and Your Organization. There are more than 110,000 opportunities with 3,100+ providers to earn PDCs, including attending events, volunteering, completing major work projects, and reading books. You can also earn recertification by retaking the certification exam.

Although you can earn all sixty credits by attending virtual or in-person professional development programs, many certified professionals also choose to document a major work project completed and endorsed by their supervisor to earn up to thirty PDCs. You can also earn up to thirty PDCs in the Advance Your Profession category. This includes things like completing a survey, making a presentation, or publishing an article or book chapter.

When you are planning your recertification strategy, don't overlook the importance of volunteering. Serving in a volunteer leadership role or even as a volunteer supporting SHRM item-writing activities for future exams is an important way to supplement your professional development education and earn PDCs.

Visit the SHRM recertification page online to learn more about recertification and other types of activities that qualify for PDCs.

 ONLINE

Learn about the various categories, what kind of documentation to submit, and how many PDCs can be earned by category: https://www.shrm.org /certification/recertification/qualifying-activities /Pages/default.aspx.

On behalf of the entire SHRM team around the globe, we wish you good luck on the SHRM certification exam. Visualize success and you can succeed!

Appendices

Appendix 1

Twenty-Five Top Test-Taking Tips

SHRM collected the top test-taking tips from SHRM-certified HR profession-als as well as subject matter experts who support the development of the exams. Use these ideas to refine your study plan and set yourself up for success on exam day!

1. Make this test your biggest priority for several months before the test!

2. Set aside time to study, and prepare your family for the time commitment proper preparation will require.

3. If you are not self-disciplined, take an in-person or virtual prep course.

4. Understand that there is *no way* to retain all the information covered in the materials. Memorize principles, not facts.

5. Connect with a learning group for the SHRM test preparation.

6. Know your study style.

7. Use practice tests and practice questions to help you prepare.

8. Understand the scenarios in order to apply the best approach.

9. Understand the concept to apply it (not just the definition).

10. Relax. If you've been in HR for any length of time, you likely have the knowledge, but don't realize it!

11. Keep a positive and open mind about the test and *know* you will pass if you take the time to read each question more than once, as well as the answers.

12. Use the SHRM Learning System—it's a great preparation tool.

13. Take your flash cards with you so you can review them whenever you have free time.

14. After studying diligently, take some time off from work the week of the exam for final review, then take a break from study the day before the exam.

15. Set an exam time when you are physically and mentally sharpest.

16. Eat a high-protein meal before your exam.

17. Approach questions as if they were your own problems. For SJIs, rely on best practice as defined in the SHRM Body of Applied Skills and Knowledge (BASK) to identify the best action to take.

18. Read the question carefully. If a question asks for an action, choose a response option that is the correct action to take. If a question asks for an approach or strategy, choose an approach or strategy accordingly as your answer.

19. Take an educated guess. There is no penalty for guessing.

20. Flag questions that you want to go back to before finishing each section.

21. Save enough time to answer flagged questions at the end of each section.

22. Remain calm and confident during the exam. Go with your gut.

23. Believe in yourself.

24. Relax. The test is asking you questions so you can show 1) what you know, 2) what you know how to do, and 3) that you can perform competently using what you know and know how to do. The questions are *not* written to trick you.

25. Celebrate no matter what happens!

Appendix 2

Forty-Item Practice Test and Answers

Introduction

This practice test includes forty test items that were previously administered on either the SHRM-CP or SHRM-SCP exams in recent years. Similar to the real exams, this practice test is divided into separate sections that are composed of either knowledge items or situational judgment items. The first section contains a total of twelve knowledge and foundational knowledge items, the second section contains sixteen situational judgment items, and the third section contains another set of twelve knowledge and foundational knowledge items.

Because this practice test only contains forty items, it is not representative of the entire blueprint that is used to build the SHRM-CP and SHRM-SCP exams. In other words, this practice test is not a "mini exam," and it does not represent all knowledge or behavioral areas tested on the exams. However, the practice test will give you a flavor of how the questions are structured on the exam and allow you to practice your testing-taking strategies as you answer them.

To get a better sense of the real exams, SHRM recommends that you take the practice items during a timed period. We suggest you allot one and a half minutes per question (sixty minutes total) to gauge your ability to answer questions under the time constraints of the real exams.

One very important caution: do not assume that ability to answer items on this forty-item practice test correctly equates to a passing score on the certification exam. Similarly, do not use the results of your performance on the practice test to predict how well you will do on the certification exam itself. This practice test is composed of less than one-third of the number of items on the SHRM-CP and SHRM-SCP exams. Also, these practice items do not fully cover all of the competency clusters and knowledge domains that are represented on the real exams.

Additionally, the conditions in your at-home or in-office environment will not match or likely mirror the controlled environment in which a SHRM exam is administered. For these reasons, the practice items are intended to give a pre-view of the structure and format of test questions. It is not appropriate to use results to predict an outcome on your exam, and doing well on the practice test is not a guarantee of a passing result on your exam. Refer to Chapter 3 for more information on scoring and exam construction of the SHRM-CP and SHRM-SCP exams.

The answer key and rationales for the correct answers for knowledge and foundational knowledge items appear at the end of the practice test. For situational judgment items, the answer key represents the best response or most effective course of action, as determined by a panel of SHRM-certified experts.

For examinees who plan to test outside of the United States: The last two questions are about US Employment Law and Regulations. Questions in this functional area do not appear on exams for examinees who reside outside of the United States. If you reside outside the United States and plan to take your exam outside of the United States, give yourself fifty-seven minutes to complete the practice test and skip the last two questions. This means you will answer thirty-eight items instead of forty items.

Good luck on the practice test!

Section 1: This section is composed of twelve knowledge items.

1. During which phase of the strategic planning process should HR allocate resources to specific actions?

   A. Formulation

   B. Development

   C. Implementation

   D. Review

2. How should an HR manager calculate monthly turnover?

   A. (Number of total monthly separations [excluding layoffs] / average number of employees on the payroll during the month) × 100

   B. (Number of unexpected separations during the year) ÷ 12

   C. (Average number of separations per month / number of employees staying per month) × 100

   D. [Number of total monthly separations (including layoffs) / average number of employees on the payroll during the month] × 100

3. Which approach to expatriate compensation is best to use if the organization's top priority is ensuring equity between expatriates and employees in the host country?

   A. Balance sheet

   B. Lump sum

   C. Localization

   D. Negotiation

4. Which statement best describes the primary rationale for why businesses choose to develop and implement a corporate social responsibility strategy?

   A. Meets required legal and regulatory standards.

   B. Leads to positive changes in attitudes and behaviors.

   C. Satisfies a moral imperative of acting as a good citizen.

   D. Results in a better understanding of issues that impact society.

5. A CEO approaches an HR director for help identifying the company's future leaders. Which should the HR director suggest?

    A. Implement an internal employee promotion program where employees can request leadership positions.

    B. Administer departmental surveys to collect input from employees.

    C. Request recommendations from the management team.

    D. Perform behavioral assessments to assess employees' personal characteristics and qualities.

6. Which consideration is most important when designing incentive programs with rewards based on improvements in work group productivity?

    A. Level of cooperativeness in the workplace

    B. Proportion of an employee's salary that is linked to variable pay

    C. Value of the incentive relative to an employee's total compensation

    D. Extent to which the incentive program significantly affects profits

7. An organization's management team is considering whether to build a manufacturing facility in another country as well as whether to introduce its products in that location. Which action should the management team take first in the decision-making process?

    A. Negotiate a merger with local supplier companies.

    B. Identify a talent source from which to recruit employees for the new facility.

    C. Assess the political climate and economic stability in the new location.

    D. Perform due diligence activities to assess potential business partners.

8. Which describes the resolution of conflict between parties during the first stage of alternative dispute resolution?

    A. An arbitrator imposes a legally binding resolution.

    B. A peer review forum uses an open panel discussion.

    C. A neutral third party provides conflict-solving ideas.

    D. A supervisor helps to create a collaborative settlement.

9. Which objective is consistent with Locke's theory when establishing goals?

   A. Answer customer queries as quickly as possible.

   B. Investigate absence levels and recommend solutions.

   C. Recruit 50 new customers before the end of the year.

   D. Carry out quarterly analyses to improve customer satisfaction.

10. Which method is used to provide on-the-job management development?

    A. Coaching

    B. Simulation

    C. Role play

    D. Conference

11. Which type of social media should an HR manager use to most effectively provide candidates with updates about organizational events and activities?

    A. Microblogging

    B. Professional networks

    C. Podcasting

    D. Content-driven communities

12. Which step is most important during the implementation of an applicant tracking system?

    A. Clarifying business processes and requirements

    B. Testing the system before implementation

    C. Choosing a user-friendly system

    D. Creating training programs for hiring managers

Section 2: This section is composed of sixteen situational judgment items.

The following scenario accompanies the next three items.

A large consumer goods company with geographically dispersed employees and a bureaucratic organizational structure seeks to create a participative and inclusive culture by requiring employees to communicate and collaborate across product lines. The company changes its existing structure by shifting work between locations, reducing the size of its management team, and eliminating a major product line. Despite these changes, employees find it difficult to develop strong relationship ties given the lack of organizational support, schedule conflicts, and strict policies. The HR manager hires an early career HR professional to explore changing the organizational culture and improving communication among employees, customers, and stakeholders across geographic locations. The HR professional proposes an employee recognition program that encourages collaborative behavior by awarding an outstanding employee with an opportunity to give a presentation to the CEO on the importance of workplace collaboration. The HR manager rejects the proposal due to concerns about the effectiveness of a presentation for fostering an inclusive work environment. Confident that recognizing collaborative behavior is the best approach to participation and inclusion, the HR professional proposes a recognition program that gives employees an opportunity to nominate collaborative employees through an HR technology system. The HR professional's approach to the employee recognition program is a unique idea, but it requires design and delivery assistance. The HR professional receives positive feedback from other early career professionals working outside of HR on the various ideas and suggestions for new approaches.

13. Which action should the HR professional take when designing a solution to change the culture across the entire company?

    A. Include feedback from focus groups to ensure that all stakeholder voices are heard and acknowledged.

    B. Link the program to the company's vision of employee collaboration across product lines and geographic locations.

    C. Recognize geographically dispersed employees who collaborate despite schedule conflicts and high travel costs.

    D. Review program details and meet with the HR manager to ensure understanding of expectations.

14. Which action is best for the HR professional to take first after concluding that the HR technology systems currently available in the company do not support the project?

    A.   Prepare a cost-benefit analysis of the survey technology platforms with the required features and request funding to support the purchase.

    B.   Determine whether the desired technology exists in other internal business units and assess the HR department's willingness to participate.

    C.   Develop a manual solution that accomplishes the same objective and ensure the availability of an employee network to complete the work.

    D.   Adapt the current HR technology design so that it supports the project and modify if needed as the program continues to grow.

15. Which action should the HR professional take to increase the level of interest in the program among employees who provide positive feedback and suggestions for new approaches?

    A.   Refer them to a page on the company's intranet containing more information about the new program.

    B.   Ask them to forward related project ideas that they are interested in working on later in the project.

    C.   Include them in an email group and send more information as the project progresses.

    D.   Share program information with them and ask them to quickly distribute that information to their co-workers.

The following scenario accompanies the next two items.

A manufacturer built a successful and stable business over the last 50 years. Its success was created by positioning itself as a manufacturer producing high-quality products at market-premium prices. Its business strategy focuses on controlling costs through integrating manufacturing at regional company facilities where components are manufactured and assembled. Recently, the company started losing market share to competitors who rely on external vendors for component parts. Because of the steady decline in market share and decreases in the overall market price for the products, the company has become less profitable. At an annual management meeting, the current business strategy is discussed with a focus on changing the competitive strategy and increasing the reliance on new technologies. The company decides to shift its business strategy and commit resources to enhancing technology integration.

16. The CEO determines that a shift in business strategy is necessary. Which action should HR take first?

     A. Engage employees in the process to make them feel part of the transition.

     B. Make day-to-day operational and transition decisions to build confidence in company leadership.

     C. Obtain critical information from staff who are knowledgeable about clients' reactions to change.

     D. Assess success periodically as the transition unfolds.

17. The HR team conducts a strengths, weaknesses, opportunities, and threats analysis. Which action should the HR team take next to support workforce development?

     A. Navigate client and customer service support staff through new product technologies.

     B. Review structural and operational changes, reward systems, and training requirements.

     C. Update compensation structure for sales and customer service representatives.

     D. Identify key employees who will participate in leading and communicating the changes.

The following scenario accompanies the next three items.

A technology startup hires 100 new employees in one month. Due to so many people being hired in such a short period of time, the small HR department is struggling to consistently onboard all the new employees. Some HR staff thoroughly explain company policies and procedures to new employees, while others do not. Managers are submitting complaints that many of the new employees lack basic knowledge about company policies and procedures, which results in lost productivity. The HR manager, who has been with the company for three months, is asked to solve this problem.

18. Which action should the HR manager take to ensure that all future new employees receive onboarding when they join the organization?

   A.   Communicate to all managers that it is their responsibility to onboard new employees.

   B.   Review onboarding procedures with HR staff to create a checklist for onboarding new employees.

   C.   Develop a central website to refer all new employees for onboarding information.

   D.   Review the current onboarding program to make necessary improvements.

19. Several new employees tell the HR manager that they made mistakes due to the lack of knowledge of procedures, and they are concerned their managers no longer trust them. How should the HR manager address their concerns?

   A.   Meet with their managers to explain the onboarding issues and how HR is correcting them.

   B.   Send a company-wide email to explain that some new employees may not be familiar with company policies and procedures.

   C.   Tell the new employees that it takes time to build trust with their managers.

   D.   Conduct team-building training for employees and their managers to build trust.

20. The HR manager decides to implement a standardized orientation process for new employees. Which is the most effective method of developing the content for the orientation?

   A.   Ask other HR professionals in the industry about the content included in their orientation processes.

   B.   Conduct a training needs analysis of new employees and include content on areas in which they consistently lack knowledge.

   C.   Ask managers in the company what information they need new employees to learn from an orientation process.

   D.   Hire an agency to conduct, review, and design a new orientation process.

The following scenario accompanies the next three items.

After a consulting company gets a demanding new project, an employee struggles to meet the increased expectations. Following a discussion about expectations with the employee, the employee's performance improves. A rumor spreads that the employee is paying a co-worker to help complete the employee's work. While this is not explicitly against company policy, the division manager wants to immediately terminate both the employees involved if the rumor is true.

21. The division manager wants to fire both employees following an investigation that confirms the rumor even though neither employee has violated company policy. How should the HR manager advise the division manager about the best course of action?

    A.   Terminate both employees for inappropriate behavior based on the evidence.

    B.   Write a new policy requiring all collaborative projects to be approved by management.

    C.   Put both employees on a performance improvement plan based on work-rule violations discovered during the investigation.

    D.   Present a proposal to leadership to create an anonymous reporting hotline.

22. Which action should HR take first to investigate the rumors?

    A.   Collect more specific information from the individual who complained.

    B.   Inform the department director of the issue.

    C.   Review the policy to see whether updates are required pending the results of the investigation.

    D.   Ask the manager which employees need to be included in the investigation.

23. The department manager thinks the employee hired the co-worker because the employee does not possess the skills required to complete the project. How should the HR manager determine each employee's skill set to use when assigning new projects?

    A.   Conduct a skills analysis of the department staff.

    B.   Assign projects to current staff and provide training to close identified skills gaps.

    C.   Implement a 360-degree review process to provide upward and downward feedback.

    D.   Hire a consultant to train the staff on the skills needed to complete the new project.

The following scenario accompanies the next two items.

A nonprofit organization implements a customer service training program as part of one of its strategic initiatives. The executive team approves hiring an external consultant to design and develop the program. The consultant conducts internal and external focus groups as part of the assessment stage. Once the development is complete, the consultant delivers the program content to a pilot group. Pilot program participants provide excellent Level 1 evaluations, and future program sessions are full.

After the pilot is complete, a new executive joins the organization. The executive questions the design and content of the training program.

24. What should the VP of HR do to satisfy the new executive's concerns?

   A.   Revise the program with new content to address the executive's concerns.

   B.   Ask executives who were involved in the program's development to explain the program design and intent.

   C.   Tell the executive the new program will be ready to implement once a new approach is developed.

   D.   Revise the organization's strategic initiatives to reduce the focus on customer service improvement.

25. The VP of HR meets with the new executive about the training program. How should the VP of HR convince the executive that the program design is sound and aligns with the strategic initiative?

   A.   Ask about the executive's concerns about the program and be prepared to address questions.

   B.   Show the executive sample participant evaluations and the overall statistical evaluation results.

   C.   Give the new executive a one-on-one session so the executive experiences the program firsthand.

   D.   Recognize the executive has already made a decision about the program design and continue as planned.

The following scenario accompanies the next three items.

A senior manager has been with a midsize company for 18 years and leads a sales office of 30 employees. The senior manager, whose team has led the company in sales for the past five years, is considered one of the company's best managers. However, the senior manager is constantly late in arriving at the office in the morning, and frequently takes two-hour lunch breaks. In performance reviews, the senior manager's supervisor has discussed the problem and given verbal warnings, but the senior manager's behavior has not changed. Recently, sales in the senior manager's office decreased by 50 percent. Consequently, the CEO asks the HR manager to address the senior manager's punctuality and performance problems immediately.

26. The CEO notifies the HR manager that the senior manager must be terminated if punctuality does not improve. What should the HR manager do next to help the senior manager improve punctuality?

    A. Send an email informing the senior manager of the consequences if punctuality does not improve.

    B. Advise the CEO to perform a time and attendance review with the senior manager.

    C. Meet with the senior manager to explain that productivity has been an issue and has lost the company money.

    D. Hold a meeting with the senior manager to inform the senior manager that continued tardiness will lead to termination.

27. When confronted about the issue, the senior manager becomes defensive. The senior manager claims that there is not a problem and that the CEO simply wants a new senior manager. How should the HR manager respond?

    A. Provide evidence of the continued punctuality problems.

    B. Share the CEO's praise for the senior manager to show the company's appreciation.

    C. Recommend counseling for the senior manager's personal defensiveness.

    D. Share another employee's time and attendance issue with the sales manager and how it was solved.

28. Which action should the HR manager have taken to prevent punctuality problems like this from continuing so long?

    A. Require all employees to record time worked and lunch breaks taken on the job.

    B. Schedule mandatory meetings at the start of the workday.

    C. Provide monthly communication on the importance of adhering to the organization's tardiness policy.

    D. Routinely monitor tardiness and immediately address the matter after initial violation.

Section 3: This section is composed of twelve knowledge items.

29. Which is an example of a bottom-line HR metric?

    A. Employee turnover costs

    B. Workplace ergonomic data

    C. HR cost per trainee

    D. HR return on investment

30. Which action most accurately reflects an HR manager's responsibility for supporting workforce planning?

    A. Creating qualified candidate pools

    B. Interviewing candidates for open positions

    C. Selecting candidates with the best organizational fit

    D. Highlighting the performance potential of best candidates

31. A company decides to transfer key project engineers to an international project site. Which step should HR take first to ensure a fair compensation system for all employees regardless of location?

    A. Design a new compensation package including merit pay for the transferred employees.

    B. Convert the engineers' salaries to the host country's currency.

    C. Provide relocation assistance to transferred employees.

    D. Implement cost-of-living adjustments for all transferred employees.

32. Which is a primary advantage of using multirater performance reviews?

    A. The reviews are easy to administer.

    B. Raters require less formal training.

    C. Feedback is more easily summarized.

    D. Bias and prejudice are minimized.

33. Which aspect of diversity, equity, and inclusion training is the most effective for resolving conflict?

    A. Negating stereotypes about group members from different backgrounds

    B. Highlighting similarities of employees from different backgrounds

    C. Encouraging employees from minority backgrounds to assimilate with the cultural majority

    D. Encouraging tolerance of employees from different backgrounds

34. When designing an employee recognition program, which approach is most effective?

    A.   Allow HR staff to decide the best ways to recognize employees.

    B.   Ask employees which behaviors they think should be recognized.

    C.   Keep the names of the design team confidential so employees do not influence them.

    D.   Maintain confidentiality about the process used to select award winners.

35. How should a manager build social capital in the workplace?

    A.   Build trust within the work unit.

    B.   Obtain advanced training in a specialized area.

    C.   Implement a bonus program for high performers.

    D.   Identify employees' roles and responsibilities clearly.

36. A company is deciding between two countries as the location for its customer service department. How should an HR manager best support the company with this decision?

    A.   Run a strengths, weakness, opportunities, and threats analysis.

    B.   Create consistency through enforcement of policies and procedures.

    C.   Source appropriate technology for the new location.

    D.   Develop a facilities plan to prepare for the upcoming move.

37. Which proactive strategy is most critical when a significant number of employees with organizational seniority and longevity are expected to retire?

    A.   Develop an outplacement program to assist these workers with transitioning to part-time work.

    B.   Offer modified work schedules to increase organizational attractiveness among applicants.

    C.   Create opportunities for these workers to mentor and transfer knowledge to junior employees.

    D.   Design ergonomic processes to prevent serious and costly workplace injuries.

38. A company's turnover analysis reveals that most employees leave the company during their second or third year of employment. Which provides the best explanation for the voluntary turnover?

   A. Compensation philosophy

   B. Employee benefit offerings

   C. Career development options

   D. Onboarding program

39. Which question can an employer legally ask an applicant in the United States?

   A. Do you have a physical or mental disability?

   B. How many times were you absent due to illness in the past two years?

   C. What was your attendance record at your last job?

   D. Have you ever filed for workers' compensation?

40. When creating an emergency action plan, which OSHA element must an HR manager include?

   A. Alternative communications center

   B. List of beneficiaries and primary care providers of all employees

   C. Description of the system used to notify employees of the need to evacuate

   D. Procedures to account for employees after an evacuation

Knowledge items have a correct response, and the situational judgment items have a best or most effective response; both are known as the *key*.

» For *knowledge and foundational knowledge items*, there is one correct answer and three incorrect answers. The rationale explains why the correct answer for each knowledge or foundational item is correct.

» Unlike knowledge-based items, *situational judgment items* have no one "correct" answer. Instead, they have degrees of effectiveness that are based on the judgment of a group of subject matter experts. While more than one of the possible strategies might be effective, one will be the best strategy based on the situation and as decided by a panel of SHRM-certified HR professionals.

Question Number	Key	Rationale
1	C	Strategy implementation is the phase during which resources are allocated to various actions included in the strategy. Resource allocation does not occur at the formulation, development, or review phases of a strategy.
2	A	Monthly turnover is accurately calculated by the formula shown in the first option. The other three calculations are either missing a factor or include a factor that is not used to calculate monthly turnover.
3	C	Localization is the best compensation approach to use when striving to achieve pay equity between expatriates on international assignment and host-country nationals already working in the country.
4	C	Corporate social responsibility (CSR) programs are primarily implemented so an organization can do good works as part of programs that benefit the local community and serve as a way of giving back to that community. While CSR programs may lead to improved attitudes and a better understanding of the community, neither is a primary reason for implementing a CSR program. CSR programs are generally not regulated; thus, implementing one to meet legal requirements is not correct.
5	D	Perform behavioral assessments to reveal employee's personal characteristics and qualities is the correct answer. Companies use behavioral assessments because the quantitative and qualitative information revealed in a behavioral assessment can be measured against the qualifications of a job. The other answers are based on opinions and volunteering for the job, rather than data.
6	A	Cooperation among team members is the most important design consideration if the organization wishes to reward group productivity. Total compensation, variable pay, and profit margins are not a consideration if the goal is to incentivize team productivity.
7	C	When considering international investments, risk assessment is key before negotiations. Mergers, due diligence, and recruitment all occur after the assessment of the risk is completed.
8	C	Alternative dispute resolution (ADR) involves a neutral third party to work toward resolution of the conflict. The first thing this neutral third party should do is suggest ideas to resolve the dispute. Peer reviewers, arbitrators, and supervisors serve different roles at different times during the ADR process, but the neutral third party takes the lead during the first stage of ADR.
9	C	Recruiting 50 new customers before the end of year has the specific and measurable components that are hallmarks of Locke's theory. The other three options are vague and do not include specific benchmarks to measure goal achievement.

Question Number	Key	Rationale
10	A	Coaching is the approach that specifically addresses on-the-job management behavior improvement. Role play, simulation, and conference may be tools used during coaching, but coaching provides the overall framework to address improvement of behavior for management team members.
11	A	Microblogging provides an efficient and expeditious way for recruiters to communicate updated information to candidates who have been identified to proceed to the next stage in the recruitment process.
12	A	System development of any kind, including for an applicant tracking system, begins by thoroughly defining a set of system specifications based on the organization's business processes and requirements. Training, selecting, and testing the system all occur at points further along in the system development process.
13	B	
14	B	
15	C	
16	A	
17	B	Situational judgment items (SJIs) require the examinee to think about what is occurring in the scenario and decide which response option identifies the most effective course of action. Other response options may be something you *could* do to respond in the situation, but SJIs require thinking and acting based on the best of the available options. Do not base your answer on your organization's approach to handling the situation but, rather, answer based on what you know *should* be done according to best practice. Panels of SHRM-certified subject matter experts rate the effectiveness of each response option, and the "best" answer is derived by statistical analysis of those expert opinions.
18	B	
19	B	
20	A	
21	B	
22	A	
23	B	
24	B	
25	A	
26	D	
27	A	
28	D	
29	D	HR return on investment (ROI) is a holistic measure of HR programs and services. The other three metrics are specifically focused on single outcomes and do not therefore address bottom-line issues like ROI does.
30	A	To support the organization's overall workforce development plans, the HR manager's most important responsibility is to develop and create a diverse pool of qualified candidates. While interviewing and selecting candidates and subsequently highlighting components of high-performing individuals are important for implementing a workforce development plan, the critical first step is to attract qualified candidates to meet the organization's workforce needs.

Question Number	Key	Rationale
31	D	Cost-of-living adjustments give the same percent increase across the board to everyone, regardless of performance and based on the actual cost of living where the organization is located. Other options may be appropriate but only after determining whether a change in base salary is needed based on the cost to live in the organization's specific location.
32	D	Multirater performance reviews combine feedback from several reviewers, which minimizes bias and prejudice. Multirater reviews take more effort to administer, require reviewer training, and require feedback to be summarized across reviewers.
33	B	In diversity, equity, and inclusion training, focusing on commonalities is best. Highlighting commonalities among employees of different backgrounds—rather than focusing on differences, requiring employees to adjust or attempting to negate stereotypes—best helps the organization resolve conflict.
34	B	To gain employee buy-in for a recognition program, it is most effective to ask employees which behaviors they think should be recognized. Allowing HR staff to decide does not build employee buy-in. Confidentiality is important in many parts of HR, but confidentiality in a recognition process may make employees feel the process is unfair or used for favoritism.
35	A	Social capital is generally defined as the value of individuals' social relationships with others. A manager can build social capital by building trust between employees in a work unit. The other options talk about building skills, increasing potential compensation, and clarifying job roles, which do not build social capital.
36	A	An HR manager should use a strengths, weaknesses, opportunities, and threats analysis to scrutinize the strategy from an HR perspective. The other actions are useful specific actions to take once a decision has been made, although sourcing technology and developing a facilities plan may be handled outside of HR.
37	C	When employees are close to retiring, the most important organizational issue to address is knowledge retention. Creating opportunities for mentorship and knowledge transfer allow the organization to retain this important asset.
38	C	Employees in their second or third year of employment are most likely to leave because of limited career development options. Employees who leave because of ineffective onboarding, limited benefit offerings, or low compensation are likely to identify these issues before or soon after joining an organization, and therefore would leave earlier in their tenure (or perhaps turn down an employment offer).
39	C	An employer can legally ask about a candidate's attendance record with a previous employer. The ADA prohibits employers from asking disability-related questions or questions that are likely to elicit information about a candidate's disability during interviews, which makes the other response options incorrect.

Question Number	Key	Rationale
40	D	OSHA provides guidance on establishing a wide variety of steps to take in response to an emergency, including establishing an alternative communication center, providing lists of medical service providers, and writing an effective announcement to motivate employees to evacuate. However, regarding the most important thing for an HR manager to include in the plan itself, that is to establish and communicate the protocol staff must use to account for every employee post-evacuation. After everyone is accounted for, other components of the plan can be implemented.

Appendix 3

Glossary of Terms Used in the Exams

The following terms appear in the SHRM Body of Applied Skills and Knowledge (SHRM BASK), may appear on the SHRM-CP and SHRM-SCP certification exams, and are applicable to all examinees.

Term	Definition
ADA *(US examinees only)*	Americans with Disabilities Act
ADAAA *(US examinees only)*	Americans with Disabilities Act Amendment Act
ADDIE	Analysis, design, development, implementation, evaluation model; a five-step instructional design framework that guides the design and development of learning programs.
ADEA *(US examinees only)*	Age Discrimination in Employment Act
ADR	Alternative dispute resolution; an umbrella term for the various approaches and techniques (other than litigation) that can be used to resolve a dispute, such as arbitration, conciliation, and mediation.
analytics	Tools that add context or subclassifying comparison groups to data so that the data can be used for decision support.
applicant	Person who applies for or formally expresses interest in a position.
arbitration	Method of alternative dispute resolution (ADR) by which disputing parties agree to be bound by the decision of one or more impartial persons to whom they submit their dispute for final determination.
assessment center	Process by which job candidates or employees are evaluated to determine suitability and/or readiness for employment, training, promotion, or an assignment.
ATS	Applicant tracking system; a software application that automates organizations' management of the recruiting process, such as accepting application materials and screening applicants.
balance sheet	Statement of an organization's financial position at a specific point in time, showing assets, liabilities, and shareholder equity.

Term	Definition
balanced scorecard	Performance management tool that depicts an organization's overall performance as measured against goals, lagging indicators, and leading indicators.
benchmarking	Process by which an organization identifies performance gaps and sets goals for performance improvement by comparing its data, performance levels, and/or processes against those of other organizations.
benefits	Mandatory or voluntary payments or services provided to employees, which typically cover retirement, health care, sick pay/disability, life insurance, and paid time off (PTO).
BFOQ *(US examinees only)*	Bona fide occupational qualification; a factor (such as gender, religion, or age) that is reasonably necessary, in the normal operations of an organization, to carry out a particular job function.
bias	A partiality or an inclination or predisposition for or against something.
business case	Tool or document that defines a specific problem, proposes a solution, and provides justifications for the proposal in terms of time, cost efficiency, and probability of success.
business intelligence	Raw data (which may be internal and/or external to an organization) that is translated into meaningful information for decision-makers to use in taking strategic action.
business unit	Element or segment of an organization that represents a specific business function, such as accounting, marketing, or production; also may be called department, division, group, cost center, or functional area.
buy-in	Process by which a person or group provides a sustained commitment in support of a decision, approach, solution, or course of action.
candidate experience	Perception of a job seeker about an employer based on interaction during the complete recruitment process.
career development	Progression through a series of employment stages characterized by relatively unique issues, themes, and tasks.
career mapping	Process by which organizations use visual tools or guides to depict prototypical or exemplary career possibilities and paths in terms of sequential positions, roles, and stages.
career pathing	Process by which employers provide employees with a clear outline for moving from a current to a desired position.
cash flow statement	Statement of an organization's ability to meet its current and short-term obligations by showing incoming and outgoing cash and cash reserves in operations, investments, and financing.
center of excellence	Team or structure that provides expertise, best practices, support, and/or knowledge transfer in a focused area.
CEO	Chief executive officer
CFO	Chief financial officer

Term	Definition
change initiative	Transition in an organization's technology, culture, or behavior of its employees and managers.
change management	Principles and practices for managing a change initiative so it is more likely to be accepted and provided with the resources (such as financial, human, physical, etc.) necessary to reshape the organization and its people.
CHRO	Chief human resource officer
coaching	Focused, interactive communication and guidance intended to develop and enhance on-the-job performance, knowledge, or behavior.
COBRA *(US examinees only)*	Consolidated Omnibus Budget Reconciliation Act
code of conduct	Document that summarizes the standards of business conduct for an organization, such as rules, values, ethical principles, and vision.
comparable worth	Concept that jobs that are primarily filled by women and require skills, effort, responsibility, and working conditions comparable to similar jobs primarily filled by men should have the same classifications and salaries.
competencies	Clusters of highly interrelated attributes, including knowledge, skills, abilities, and other characteristics (KSAOs) that give rise to the behaviors needed to perform a given job effectively.
compliance	State of being in accordance with all national, federal, regional, and/or local laws, regulations and/or other government author-ities and requirements applicable to the places in which an organization operates.
conciliation	Method of nonbinding alternative dispute resolution (ADR) by which a neutral third party tries to help disputing parties reach a mutually agreeable decision, such as mediation.
conflict of interest	Situation in which a person or organization may potentially benefit, either directly or indirectly, from undue influence due to involvement in outside activities, relationships, or investments that conflict with or have an impact on the employment relation-ship or its outcomes.
COO	Chief operating officer
cost-benefit analysis	Approach to determining the financial impact of an organiza-tion's activities and programs on profitability by comparing value created against the cost of creating that value.
critical path	Amount of time needed to complete all required elements or components of a task, which is determined by taking into ac-count all project-task relationships.
CSR	Corporate social responsibility; an organization's commitment to operate ethically and contribute to economic development while improving the quality of life of the workforce and their families as well as of the local and global community.

Term	Definition
culture	Basic beliefs, attitudes, values, behaviors, and customs shared and followed by members of a group, which give rise to the group's sense of identity.
diversity	The differences between individuals on any attribute that may lead to the perception that another person is different from the self.
due diligence	Requirement to thoroughly investigate an action before it is taken through diligent research and evaluation.
EAP	Employee assistance program
EEOC (US examinees only)	Equal Employment Opportunity Commission
e-learning	Electronic media delivery of educational and training materials, processes, and programs.
emotional intelligence	Ability to be aware of, control, and express one's emotions, and to handle interpersonal relationships judiciously and empathetically.
employee engagement	Employees' emotional commitment to an organization, which is demonstrated by their willingness to put in discretionary effort to promote the organization's effective functioning.
employee experience	Sum of all touchpoints an employee has with an employer, including those related to an employee's role, workspace, manager, and well-being.
employee surveys	Instruments that collect and assess information on employees' attitudes and perceptions of the work environment or employment conditions, such as engagement or job satisfaction.
employees	Persons who exchange their work for wages or salary.
EPA (US examinees only)	Equal Pay Act
equality	Equal treatment of individuals and groups.
equity	A relative form of equality that takes into consideration the needs and characteristics of the individuals, the context of the situation, and circumstances that result in disparate outcomes.
ERISA (US examinees only)	Employee Retirement Income Security Act
ethics	Set of behavioral guidelines that an organization expects employees at all levels to follow to ensure appropriate moral and ethical business standards.
evidence-based	Approach to evaluation and decision-making that utilizes data and research findings to drive business outcomes.
EVP	Employee value proposition; employees' perceived value of the total rewards and tangible and intangible benefits they receive from the organization as part of employment, which drives unique and compelling organizational strategies for talent acquisition, retention, and engagement.

Term	Definition
exit interview	Meeting held with an employee who is about to leave an organization, typically to discuss the employee's reasons for leaving and the employee's experience of working for the organization.
FCRA *(US examinees only)*	Fair Credit Reporting Act
FLSA *(US examinees only)*	Fair Labor Standards Act
FMLA *(US examinees only)*	Family and Medical Leave Act
focus group	Small group of invited persons (typically six to twelve people) who actively participate in a structured discussion in which a facilitator elicits input on a specific product, process, policy, or program.
gap analysis	Method of assessing a current state to determine what is needed to move to a desired future state.
gig economy	Free market system in which temporary positions are common and organizations hire independent workers for short-term commitments instead of full-time employees.
GINA *(US examinees only)*	Genetic Information Nondiscrimination Act
globalization	Status of growing interconnectedness and interdependency among countries, people, markets, and organizations worldwide.
governance	System of rules and processes set up by an organization to ensure its compliance with local and international laws, accounting rules, ethical norms, internal codes of conduct, and other standards.
hazard	Potential harm that is often associated with a condition or activity that, if left uncontrolled, can result in injury or damage to persons or property.
HIPAA *(US examinees only)*	Health Insurance Portability and Accountability Act
HR	Human resources
HR service model	Approach to structuring and delivering an organization's HR services to support organizational success.
HRBP	HR business partner; an HR professional who advises an organization's leaders in developing and implementing a human capital strategy that closely aligns with overall organizational mission, vision, and goals.
HRIS	Human resource information system used for gathering, storing, maintaining, retrieving, revising, and reporting relevant HR data.
HRM	Human resource management
inclusion	Extent to which each person in an organization is and feels welcomed, respected, supported, and valued as a team member.

Term	Definition
individual development plan	Document that guides employees toward their goals for professional development and growth.
information management	Use of technology to collect, process, and condense information for the purpose of managing the information efficiently as an organizational resource.
integrity	Adherence to a set of ethical standards that reflect strong moral principles, honesty, and consistency in behavior.
IT	Information technology
job analysis	Process of systematically studying a job to identify the activities/tasks and responsibilities it includes, the personal qualifications necessary to perform it, and the conditions under which it is performed.
job description	Document that describes a job and its essential functions and requirements, such as knowledge, skills, abilities, tasks, reporting structure, and responsibilities.
job enlargement	Process of broadening a job's scope by adding different tasks to the job.
job enrichment	Process of increasing a job's depth by adding responsibilities to the job.
job evaluation	Process of determining a job's value and price to attract and retain employees by comparing the job against other jobs within the organization or against similar jobs in competing organizations.
KPI	Key performance indicator; a quantifiable measure of performance that gauges an organization's progress toward strategic objectives or other agreed-upon performance standards.
KSAOs	Knowledge, skills, abilities, and other characteristics.
labor union	Group of workers who formally organize and coordinate their activities to achieve common goals in their relationship with an employer or group of employers, such as a trade union.
lagging indicator	Type of metric describing an activity or change in performance that has already occurred.
leadership	Ability to influence, guide, inspire, or motivate a group or person to achieve their goals.
leadership development	Interventions designed to help an individual gain the knowledge, skills, abilities, and other characteristics (KSAOs) to engage with people and persuade them to work toward a vision or goal.
leading indicator	Type of metric describing an activity that can change future performance and predict success in the achievement of strategic goals.
liabilities	Organization's debts and other financial obligations.
LMRA *(US examinees only)*	Labor Management Relations Act

Term	Definition
M&A	Merger and acquisition; a process by which two separate organizations combine, either by joining together as relative equals (merger) or by one procuring the other (acquisition).
manager development	Interventions designed to help an individual gain the knowledge, skills, abilities, and other characteristics (KSAOs) required to manage people and resources to deliver a product or service.
measurement	Process of collecting, quantifying, and evaluating data.
mediation	Method of nonbinding alternative dispute resolution (ADR) by which a neutral third party tries to help disputing parties reach a mutually agreeable decision, such as conciliation.
mentoring	Relationship in which one person helps guide another's development.
mission statement	Concise outline of an organization's strategy that specifies the activities it intends to pursue and the course its management has charted for the future.
MNC	Multinational corporation
motivation	Factors that initiate, direct, and sustain human behavior over time.
negotiation	Process by which two or more parties work together to reach agreement on a matter.
NLRA *(US examinees only)*	National Labor Relations Act
offshoring	Method by which an organization relocates its processes or production to an international location through subsidiaries or third-party affiliates.
onboarding	Process of integrating a new employee with a company and its culture, as well as getting a new hire the tools and information needed to become a productive member of the team.
organizational effectiveness	Degree to which an organization is successful in executing its strategic objectives and mission.
organizational learning	Acquisition and/or transfer of knowledge within an organization through activities or processes that may occur at several organizational levels. Ability of an organization to learn from its mistakes and adjust its strategy accordingly.
organizational values	Beliefs and principles defined by an organization to direct and govern its employees' behavior.
orientation	Process by which new employees become familiar with the organization and with their specific department, co-workers, and job.
OSHA *(US examinees only)*	Occupational Safety and Health Act (law) Occupational Safety and Health Administration (agency)
outsourcing	Process by which an organization contracts with third-party vendors to provide selected services or activities instead of hiring new employees.

Term	Definition
performance appraisal	Process of measuring and evaluating an employee's adherence to performance standards and providing feedback to the employee.
performance management	Tools, activities, and processes that an organization uses to manage, maintain, and/or improve the job performance of employees.
performance measures	Data or calculations comparing current performance against key performance indicators (KPIs).
performance standards	Behaviors and results defined by an organization to communicate the expectations of management.
PESTLE	Political, economic, social, technological, legal, and environmental analysis; a method used to assess external factors and their influence on an organization.
position	Scope of work roles and responsibilities associated with one or more persons.
PTO	Paid time off
realistic job preview	Tool used in the staffing/selection process to provide an applicant with honest, complete information about the job and work environment.
recruitment	Process by which an organization seeks out candidates and encourages them to apply for job openings.
regulation	Rule or order issued by an administrative agency of government, which usually has the force of law.
reliability	Extent to which a measurement instrument provides consistent results.
remediation	Process by which an unacceptable action or behavior is corrected.
remote work	Work that is completed away from a company's office or other dedicated workspace (also known as telework).
remuneration	Total pay in the form of salary and wages received in exchange for employment, such as allowances, benefits, bonuses, cash incentives, and monetary value of noncash incentives.
remuneration surveys	Instruments that collect information on prevailing market compensation and benefits practices, such as base pay, pay ranges, starting wage rates, statutory and market cash payments, paid time off (PTO), and variable compensation.
repatriation	Process by which employees returning from international assignments reintegrate into their home country's culture, conditions, and employment.
restructuring	Act of reorganizing the legal, ownership, operational, or other structures of an organization.
retention	Ability of an organization to keep its employees.
risk	Uncertainty that has an effect on an objective, where the effect may include opportunities, losses, and threats.

Term	Definition
risk management	System for identifying, evaluating, and controlling actual and potential risks to an organization, which typically incorporates mitigation and/or response strategies, including the use of insurance.
ROI	Return on investment; data or calculation comparing an investment's monetary or intrinsic value against expended resources.
selection	Process of evaluating the most suitable candidates for a position.
sense of belonging	Extent to which individuals feel that they are a part of, included in, and connected with people at their organization.
shared services	Self-service or call center operations that promote HR expertise and deliver improved services across an organization.
Six Sigma/ Lean Six Sigma	A set of techniques and tools for process improvement that aim to increase quality by decreasing defects in processes. Lean Six Sigma also aims at increasing speed by eliminating waste.
social media	Internet technology platforms and communities that people and organizations use to communicate and share information, opinions, and resources.
socialization	Process by which persons learn the knowledge, language, social skills, culture, and values of a group or organization.
sourcing	Process by which an organization generates a pool of qualified job applicants.
stakeholders	Persons affected by an organization's social, environmental, and economic impact, such as customers, employees, local communities, regulators, shareholders, and suppliers.
stay interviews	Structured conversations with employees for the purpose of determining which aspects of a job encourage employee retention or may be improved to encourage retention, such as culture, engagement, leadership, organization, and satisfaction.
strategic management	System of actions that leaders take to drive an organization toward its goals and objectives.
strategic planning	Process of setting goals and designing a path toward organizational success.
strategy	Plan of action for accomplishing an organization's overall and long-range goals.
succession planning	Process of implementing a talent management strategy to identify and foster the development of high-potential employees or other job candidates who, over time, may move into leadership positions of increased responsibility.
sustainability	Practice of purchasing and using resources wisely by balancing economic, social, and environmental concerns toward the goal of securing present and future generations' interests.
SWOT	Strengths, weaknesses, opportunities, and threats analysis; a method for assessing an organization's strategic capabilities through the environmental scanning process, which identifies and considers the internal and external factors that affect the achievement of organizational goals and objectives.

Term	Definition
systems thinking	Process for understanding how seemingly independent units within a larger entity interact with and influence one another.
talent management	System of integrated HR processes for attracting, developing, engaging, and retaining employees who have the knowledge, skills, abilities, and other characteristics (KSAOs) to meet current and future business needs.
totalization agreements	Bilateral agreements between countries that are created for the purpose of eliminating double taxation of employees on international assignments.
training	Process by which employees are provided with the knowledge, skills, abilities, and other characteristics (KSAOs) specific to a task or job.
transformational leadership	Leadership style that focuses on challenging and developing members of an organization to attain long-range results through continuous evolution, improvement, or change based on the leader's vision and strategy.
transparency	Extent to which an organization's agreements, dealings, information, practices, and transactions are open to disclosure and review by relevant persons.
turnover	Rate at which employees leave a workforce.
ULP *(US examinees only)*	Unfair labor practice; a violation of employee rights that is prohibited under US labor-relations statutes.
unfair labor practice	A violation of employee rights that is prohibited under global labor-relations statutes.
validity	Extent to which a measurement instrument measures what it is intended to measure.
value	Measure of usefulness, worth, or importance.
variance analysis	Statistical method for identifying the degree of difference between planned and actual performance or outcomes.
vision	Description of what an organization hopes to attain and accomplish in the future, which guides it toward that defined direction.
VP	Vice president
WARN Act *(US examinees only)*	Worker Adjustment and Retraining Notification Act
work/life integration	Approach to create harmony among all areas of life, such as work, home/family, community, personal well-being, and health.
workforce planning	Strategic process by which an organization analyzes its current workforce and determines the steps required for it to prepare for future needs.
workspace solution	Modification of a job, job site, or way of doing a job so an individual with a disability has equal access to opportunity in all aspects of work and is able to perform a job's essential functions.

Appendix 4

List of Acronyms

The following acronyms appear in the SHRM Body of Applied Skills and Knowledge (SHRM BASK), may appear on the SHRM-CP and SHRM-SCP certification exams, and are applicable to all examinees.

There are three categories of acronyms—terms that are never spelled out and always appear as an acronym, are standard across HR practice, and are commonly understood by HR practitioners; common acronyms used in HR practice that are spelled out the first time they appear in a test item and then used as an acronym in the item thereafter; and terms that are likely to only be familiar to some HR professionals and therefore are always spelled out.

Category 1: Acronyms that are never spelled out: CEO, CFO, HR, HRIS, IT, and VP.

Category 2: Common terms. On the exam, each of these terms is spelled out the first time it is used in an exam item. Its acronym will be shown in parentheses if the term is used again in that item; if the term is used only once in that item, no acronym will be shown.

ADDIE	analysis, design, development, implementation, evaluation
ADR	alternative dispute resolution
ATS	applicant tracking system
CHRO	chief human resource officer
COO	chief operating officer
CSR	corporate social responsibility
EAP	employee assistance program
EVP	employee value proposition
HRBP	HR business partner
HRM	human resource management
KPI	key performance indicator
KSAOs	knowledge, skills, abilities, and other characteristics

M&A	merger and acquisition
MNC	multinational corporation
PESTLE	political, economic, social, technological, legal, and environmental
PTO	paid time off
ROI	return on investment
SWOT	strengths, weaknesses, opportunities, and threats

Note: For situational judgment items, the term will be spelled out and the acronym placed in parentheses the first time it is used in the scenario associated with that item. Then it will appear only as an acronym in the rest of the scenario and in each of the associated questions and possible responses.

Category 3: If SHRM has not included a term you or your organization typically use as an acronym on one of these preceding two lists, the term will be spelled out whenever it is used on the exam. This includes, but is not limited to, *cost-benefit analysis, center of excellence, emotional intelligence, individual development plan, information management, learning management system, realistic job preview,* and *research and development.*

Additional US Employment Law Acronyms for US-based Examinees

The following acronyms are US-specific laws, regulations, or terminology that should be familiar to all US-based examinees. These terms will only appear as acronyms on exams for US-based examinees and will not be spelled out anywhere on the exams. Examinees who are outside of the United States do not need to be familiar with these terms.

ADA	Americans with Disabilities Act
ADAAA	Americans with Disabilities Act Amendment Act
ADEA	Age Discrimination in Employment Act
BFOQ	Bona Fide Occupational Qualification
COBRA	Consolidated Omnibus Budget Reconciliation Act
EEOC	Equal Employment Opportunity Commission
EPA	Equal Pay Act
ERISA	Employee Retirement Income Security Act
FCRA	Fair Credit Reporting Act
FLSA	Fair Labor Standards Act

FMLA   Family and Medical Leave Act

GINA   Genetic Information Nondiscrimination Act

HIPAA   Health Insurance Portability and Accountability Act

LMRA   Labor Management Relations Act

NLRA   National Labor Relations Act

OSHA   Occupational Safety and Health Act *(law)* or Administration *(agency)*

ULP   Unfair Labor Practice

WARN   Worker Adjustment and Retraining Notification

Appendix 5

Online Resources

These online resources may be helpful to you as you study for the SHRM certification exams.

About the SHRM Certification Exams

SHRM Body of Applied Skills and Knowledge (BASK)
https://www.shrm.org/certification/about/body-of-competency
-and-knowledge/Pages/default.aspx

Eligibility Requirements for the SHRM-CP and SHRM-SCP Exams
https://www.shrm.org/certification/apply/EligibilityCriteria/Pages
/default.aspx

Recertification
https://www.shrm.org/certification/recertification/Pages
/Recertification-At-a-Glance.aspx

Which Exam to Take and Sample SHRM-CP Questions
https://www.shrm.org/certification/apply/eligibility-criteria/Pages
/which-exam-to-take.aspx

SHRM Membership and Communities
https://www.shrm.org/about-shrm/Pages/Membership.aspx

Preparing and Studying

SHRM Learning System
https://www.shrm.org/certification/prepare/Pages/default.aspx

Honey and Mumford Learning Styles
https://www.open.edu/openlearn/ocw/pluginfile.php/629607/mod
_resource/content/1/t175_4_3.pdf

VAK/VARK Model
https://vark-learn.com/introduction-to-vark/the-vark-modalities/

Mind Mapping
https://www.sheffield.ac.uk/ssid/301/study-skills/everyday-skills
/mind-mapping

Active Recall
https://www.brainscape.com/academy/active-recall-definition-studying/

The Leitner System
https://www.virtualsalt.com/learn10.html

Feynman Technique
https://evernote.com/blog/learning-from-the-feynman-technique/

Chunking
https://www.verywellmind.com/chunking-how-can-this-technique
-improve-your-memory-2794969

Managing Test Anxiety and Procrastination

These articles and presentations offer various viewpoints on why we procrastinate as well as tips for overcoming it.

Why We Choke Under Pressure—and How to Avoid It
https://www.ted.com/talks/sian_leah_beilock_why_we_choke_under
_pressure_and_how_to_avoid_it

Overcoming Test Anxiety
https://einsteinmed.org/education/student-affairs/academic
-support-counseling/medical-school-challenges/test-anxiety.aspx

Why You Procrastinate (It Has Nothing to Do with Self-Control)
https://www.nytimes.com/2019/03/25/smarter-living/why-you
-procrastinate-it-has-nothing-to-do-with-self-control.html

Procrastination
https://www.psychologytoday.com/us/basics/procrastination

5 Research-Based Strategies for Overcoming Procrastination
https://hbr.org/2017/10/5-research-based-strategies-for
-overcoming-procrastination

Preparing for Test Day: All About Prometric Test Centers

What to Expect
https://www.prometric.com/test-takers/what-expect

Test Center Policies
https://www.prometric.com/covid-19-update/test-center-policies

Frequently Asked Questions (FAQs)
https://www.prometric.com/test-takers/frequently-asked-questions

Exam Tutorial
https://www.prometric.com/sites/default/files/SHRM-Tutorial/launch
_assessment_delivery.html

About SHRM Books

SHRM Books develops and publishes insights, ideas, strategies, and solutions on the topics that matter most to human resource professionals, people managers, and students.

The strength of our program lies in the expertise and thought leadership of our authors to educate, empower, elevate, and inspire readers around the world.

Each year SHRM Books publishes new titles covering contemporary human resource management issues, as well as general workplace topics. With more than one hundred titles available in print, digital, and audio formats, SHRM's books can be purchased through SHRMStore.org and a variety of book retailers.

Learn more at SHRMBooks.org.

Index